People with mental illness

Author: Stewart, Gail
Reading Level: 6.0 UG
Point Value: 4.0
ACCELERATED READER QUIZ 66965

JOHN HAY MEDIA CENTER
THEotherAMERICA

People with Mental Illness

by Gail B. Stewart

Photographs by
Carl Franzén

**LUCENT
BOOKS®**

San Diego • Detroit • New York • San Francisco • Cleveland
New Haven, Conn. • Waterville, Maine • London • Munich

THOMSON
———∗———™
GALE

Cover design: Carl Franzén

The opinions of and stories told by the people in this book are entirely their own. The author has presented their accounts in their own words and has not verified their accuracy. Thus, the author can make no claim as to the objectivity of their accounts.

LIBRARY OF CONGRESS CATALOGING-IN-PUBLICATION DATA

Stewart, Gail, 1949–
   People with mental illness / by Gail B. Stewart.
     p. cm. — (The Other America series)
  Summary: Presents the personal stories of four people with mental illness, discussing how each handles the daily demands of family, education, social life, and medical treatment and finds the strength and courage to continue the battle against this common debilitating condition.
  Includes bibliographical references and index.
   ISBN 1-59018-237-5
   1. Mental illness—Juvenile literature. [1. Mental illness.] I.Title.
   RC460.2 .S746 2003
   616.89'0092'2—dc21

                                    2002007602

Printed in the United States of America

Contents

FOREWORD   4

INTRODUCTION   6
The Facts About People with Mental Illness

BRUCE   12
Bruce, a divorced father of two daughters, has bipolar disorder. He resents the way his illness has created havoc in his life.

MIKE   32
Mike suffers from schizotypal personality disorder. He experiences feelings of being persecuted and has difficulties forming relationships.

JOANN   52
Joann, a mother of three who also has a demanding job as a nurse practitioner, has experienced episodes of psychosis that included hallucinations and deep depression.

MEGAN   71
In her mid-twenties, Megan hid her symptoms of obsessive-compulsive disorder from family and friends before receiving treatment.

EPILOGUE   89

WAYS YOU CAN GET INVOLVED   90

FOR FURTHER READING   92

INDEX   93

ABOUT THE AUTHOR   95

ABOUT THE PHOTOGRAPHER   96

Foreword

O, YES,
I SAY IT PLAIN,
AMERICA NEVER WAS AMERICA TO ME.
AND YET I SWEAR THIS OATH—
AMERICA WILL BE!
    LANGSTON HUGHES

Perhaps more than any other nation in the world, the United States represents an ideal to many people. The ideal of equality—of opportunity, of legal rights, of protection against discrimination and oppression. To a certain extent, this image has proven accurate. But beneath this ideal lies a less idealistic fact—many segments of our society do not feel included in this vision of America.

They are the outsiders—the homeless, the elderly, people with AIDS, teenage mothers, gang members, prisoners, and countless others. When politicians and the media discuss society's ills, the members of these groups are defined as what's wrong with America; they are the people who need fixing, who need help, or increasingly, who need to take more responsibility. And as these people become society's fix-it problem, they lose all identity as individuals and become part of an anonymous group. In the media and in our minds, these groups are identified by condition—a disease, crime, morality, poverty. Their condition becomes their identity, and once this occurs, in the eyes of society, they lose their humanity.

The Other America series reveals the members of these groups as individuals. Through in-depth interviews, each person tells his or her unique story. At times these stories are painful, revealing individuals who are struggling to maintain their integrity, their humanity, their lives, in the face of fear, loss, and economic and spiritual hardship. At other times, their tales are exasperating, demonstrating a litany of poor choices, shortsighted thinking, and self-gratification. Nevertheless, their identities remain distinct, their personalities diverse.

As we listen to the people of *The Other America* series describe their experiences, they cease to be stereotypically defined and become tangible, individual. In the process, we may begin to understand more profoundly and think more critically about society's problems. When politicians debate, for example, whether the homeless problem is due to a poor economy or lack of initiative, it will help to read the words of the homeless. Perhaps then we can see the issue more clearly. The family who finds itself temporarily homeless because it has always been one paycheck from poverty is not the same as the mother of six who has been chronically chemically dependent. These people's circumstances are not all of one kind, and perhaps we, after all, are not so very different from them. Before we can act to solve the problems of the Other America, we must be willing to look down their path, to see their faces. And perhaps in doing so, we may find a piece of ourselves as well.

Introduction

The Facts About People with Mental Illness

Trent is thirty-two, but he has never held a job, has never married, and says that, since the age of eighteen, he has not had any friends. Although he is very bright (during elementary school, his parents were told that he was gifted), Trent suffers from schizophrenia, a disease that makes it impossible to distinguish what is real and what is only in his mind. He hears voices, sees bright lights and colors that aren't really there, and imagines that his relatives are trying to kill him.

Marci, age twenty-one, tried to commit suicide twice last year. She was on the dance line in college and had been active in her sorority. However, she has clinical depression, and sometimes has difficulty even getting out of bed in the morning. No longer able to attend classes regularly, Marci recently decided to drop out of college until she can deal with her illness.

Nick, forty-nine, suffers from bipolar disorder. His moods swing violently and unpredictably between two extremes. "Either I'm really hyper, really loud and pushy, or else I'm completely depressed," he says. He has had trouble keeping jobs, especially those that put him in contact with the public. "If I'm hyper, I am very critical. I pick fights with customers," he admits. "And when I'm in the low end, I'm totally ill at ease around people."

More Prevalent than Asthma

All three of these debilitating conditions are types of mental illness. Mental illnesses are disorders that primarily affect a person's thoughts, moods, or behavior. They can strike children, the elderly, and anyone in between. It makes no difference if a person is educated or not. It does not matter what kind of work one does or how much money one makes.

Mental illnesses are common. The American Psychiatric Association estimated in 1995 that 23 percent of Americans struggle with

6

some type of mental illness during their lifetime. Five percent of adult Americans suffer from serious mental illness, a disorder that is debilitating or persistent. Serious mental illness also affects an estimated 13 percent of children between the ages of nine and seventeen.

Mental illness is more common than cancer, asthma, or diabetes, and it cost the United States more than $180 billion in 1990 (the most recent year for which statistics are available). A little over one-third of that amount was for direct health care costs, such as hospital stays. The remainder reflects the cost of social services such as counseling and therapy, disability payments, and the lost productivity of workers with mental illness.

MISUNDERSTOOD

As common as mental illness is in the United States, it remains one of the most misunderstood diseases. Many people who suffer from a mental illness complain that the "mental" part of the term gives the public the wrong idea—that mental illness is only in the minds of the sufferers or that they are simply crazy.

Experts agree, adding that people have had incorrect notions about mental illness for centuries. In the sixteenth and seventeenth centuries, for example, people with such illnesses were locked away in asylums, where they were often beaten with whips or chains. In the 1700s, people with mental illnesses were commonly believed to be evil, and were often tortured and burned at the stake as witches. It wasn't until the end of the eighteenth century that some called for more compassionate treatment of people with mental illnesses.

Advances in treatment made a significant difference in how mental illness was viewed by the public. In the 1950s, the first tranquilizer was produced. No one was sure how or why it worked, but it was clear that the medication did help calm those who were overly anxious. Soon, other medications were developed that were effective in easing some of the symptoms of other mentally ill patients such as feelings of depression or panic. Since the illnesses responded dramatically to these drugs, the medical community began to revise their earlier thinking and view mental illnesses as true biological illnesses.

SCARY OR FUNNY?

Even though medical doctors were changing their earlier misconceptions about mental illness, the public's view of the mentally ill had not changed. To some people, "mental illness" conjured up the image of a wild-eyed, scary predator, someone who was more like a dangerous animal than a person.

For others, the term brought to mind a person whose problems were almost comic. Monroe, age forty, says that his mother suffered from an illness called obsessive-compulsive disorder. She felt nervous unless she constantly repeated certain tasks such as washing her hands or wiping the counter, which she would sometimes perform hundreds of times during the day.

"I remember seeing people on TV that did stuff like that in comedy sketches," Monroe says. "Just doing something over and over, like they forgot they did it. But it sure wasn't funny to us—we saw how that disease made my mother's life miserable."

"WE FEAR THE LOSS OF CONTROL"

Many psychologists insist that people don't mean to laugh at or trivialize mental illness. The problem is that illnesses that cause people to behave in ways that are strange are frightening.

"The thing is, if you're on the bus and you see a guy talking to himself in a loud voice, you might chuckle about it with your friend," says one therapist. "But all the while, you feel ill at ease. It's odd being around people who are seeing things or hearing things. I think it's because we fear the loss of control—we might fear the same thing could happen to us. We worry about what our friends would think, or how we could ever explain why we were having a public conversation with ourselves. Losing touch with what is real is a very frightening concept.

"I asked a class of teenagers once, if they were given a choice of a disease, if they'd rather have diabetes or some mental illness where they experienced psychotic episodes like [talking to themselves]. Both are manageable with medications. And it was interesting. The overwhelming majority said they'd rather have diabetes. It's more understood. To them, it was somehow more socially 'OK' to be sick with that than with a mental illness."

CHEMICALS AND BAD CIRCUITS

Another part of the misunderstanding is that far more is known about illnesses such as diabetes, arthritis, and cancer. Far more research dollars have been spent over the years on those diseases than on schizophrenia, for example, or bipolar disorder. Nevertheless, science has made some exciting progress regarding such illnesses, which slowly changes the way people view mental illness.

The most important progress has been the realization that, although mental illnesses affect behavior and thinking, they are caused by physical problems. Just as a pancreas that misfunctions and produces the wrong amount of insulin causes someone to become diabetic, the wrong balance of chemicals or faulty wiring in the brain can cause schizophrenia or clinical depression.

Knowing that mental illnesses have physical causes, although important, is only a first step in curing them. The brain is astoundingly complex, with more than 100 billion nerve cells, all of which are linked into thousands of circuits. The communication among the cells is accomplished by a combination of chemicals and electronic impulses, but as yet, no one knows exactly how such communication occurs or how it can go awry. According to Steven Hyman of the National Institute of Mental Health, "Understanding the normal function of the human brain—and what goes wrong in the production of serious mental illness—may be the most difficult and complex activity ever undertaken."

REASONS FOR OPTIMISM

Despite the complexity involved in understanding the human brain, experts are hopeful, for new discoveries are being made all the time. For instance, a new scanning device can pinpoint in brilliant colors the areas of the brain where nerve cells are working the hardest. Scans of schizophrenic patients in the midst of hallucinations show clearly the overactive areas that seem to cause such symptoms. The scanner has been useful in showing the area of the brain affected by obsessive-compulsive disorder as well.

Medications have also improved a great deal. Although early drugs were somewhat effective, they had a tendency to overmedicate the patient. But as researchers have learned more about the chemicals within the brain, they have been able to make more specific medicines that are effective without producing side effects. That's important, because psychiatrists know that if a prescribed medication causes dizziness, nausea, or other unpleasant symptoms, the patient won't take it.

Scientists are intrigued by the relationship between genetics and mental illness. Studies at the University of Pittsburgh, for example, found the same mutation in the DNA of ten different schizophrenic patients. Further exploration narrowed the flaw to one particular chromosome. Experts believe that discoveries like this one can lead to even better medications—or possibly cures—in the future.

For Now

For now, however, people with mental illness are usually resigned to the idea that they will never be cured. Their hope is that the medications they are prescribed will be effective enough to block the symptoms that make their lives hellishly difficult at times. Despite the medications, though, it is not unusual for some patients to experience "breakthrough" symptoms, signs of their illness that seem to overpower the drugs they take. When that occurs, says one man with bipolar disorder, "It's back to the drawing board for me. I just hope my doctor can come up with a stronger dose, a new medication, whatever it takes."

Many mentally ill people, however, are not taking medication. Having alienated family and friends and being unable to hold a job because of their disease, many have ended up on the streets. In fact, the mentally ill make up a large portion of the homeless population in the United States. Many homeless people suffering from mental illness deal with the unpleasant symptoms by turning to drugs or alcohol, which makes their illness worse. They don't have psychiatrists or access to health insurance for expensive medications. "Even if a lot of the people I see had medication," says one worker in a homeless shelter, "they'd never remember to take it, or they'd sell the pills on the street."

Four Stories

The four people whose stories make up *The Other America: People with Mental Illness* are a varied group. Bruce, who suffers from bipolar disorder, has been in and out of hospitals during much of his adult life. Although he is divorced, he feels that his relationship with his two daughters has given him strength. Even so, he feels bad that he has missed so much of his life because of his illness.

Mike has symptoms of paranoia, and has experienced frequent hostile episodes during which he is certain that other people are out to get him. Underemployed and living in a controlled environment after being confined for substance abuse, Mike says he has no plans for the future, nor does he want any.

A busy wife, mother, and nurse practitioner, Joann has had several bouts with what is called atypical depression. She has experienced vivid, often violent hallucinations and deep depression, and even sank into a catatonic state in which she lost all touch with reality and was incapable of doing anything for herself.

Finally, Megan is a young woman who has been leading a secret life with obsessive-compulsive disorder. Though on medication, she admits that it still can take her up to two hours to leave the house in the morning because she has to check and recheck (sometimes up to one hundred times) doors and electrical appliances.

These individuals vary in the severity of their diseases, the amount of support they have from family and friends, and the type of medical care they receive. However, they are all in the process of trying to understand their illnesses, trying to learn what is possible (and what is not), what symptoms can disappear with medication someday, and what they'll just have to learn to live with.

Bruce

"I CAN REMEMBER BEING IN THE
HOSPITAL, THE DOCTORS DOING
TESTS ON ME, AND IT SEEMED
LIKE I'D NEVER GET OUT."

Bruce is very nervous. It isn't that he doesn't want to talk about his mental illness, he says. It's just that he doubts whether what he has to say will be interesting to anyone.

"I'm a pretty ordinary guy," he says in a quiet voice.

"SOMETIMES PEOPLE LOOK AT ME FUNNY"

Bruce is a middle-aged father of two daughters, who are "the most important things in my life," he says proudly. He suffers from bipolar disorder, which has created havoc in his life since he was a teenager.

"I'm on medications—have been for years and years," Bruce explains. "And I have to tell you something; I just didn't want you wondering about something. I have this permanent side effect from the medicine. If you see me going like this, pulling my chin down towards my chest, you know?"

He demonstrates, doing a quick muscle twitch. "Then you know. There's a name for it, but most people wouldn't know what it means, you know? It's like a muscle tightening. Some people get it in their hands; others, a shoulder. Me—I get it in my neck."

Bruce takes a deep breath and goes on. "Sometimes I don't even really feel it; it's just that I have a reflex to kind of stretch that muscle out when it happens," he says. "So don't think it's anything strange. If I knew how to stop it, I would. Sometimes people look at me funny when I'm doing it, and they probably wonder about me. Anyway, that's what I was going to tell you."

He finishes his sentence and looks perplexed. "Am I doing this right?" he asks. "Is this what you wanted to know?"

A Different Name

When asked about bipolar disorder, Bruce smiles. "You know, for years the doctors just said I was manic-depressive. That's the term I always heard. I hear people talking now about bipolar, and I guess it's the same thing. I just don't really know why they changed the name.

"But it's a strange disease. I mean, you get the lows—the deep, deep depressions. And you get the highs—those are euphoric, where you're so full of energy and excitement you can't believe it. But the thing is, when you get one of those real manic highs, if you don't catch it on the way down, you really go into a bad depression. It's like a deep pit, like there's no way out.

"It's pretty easy to tell when a bipolar person is on a high—at least for me. I get loud; I've had people ask me why I'm talking so fast and so loud. That's how I get. In fact, I had a foreman on a job once who told me I should go see a doctor. He thought I was

Bruce has suffered from bipolar disorder since he was a teenager. This disorder brings about alternating periods of depression or euphoria.

really having mood swings, you know? Anyway, that was a long time ago, back when I was in my twenties."

"Maybe I Just Misunderstood"

Bruce says he talked with a doctor about his mood swings. "He didn't do any tests or anything," he explains. "He just sat me down and we talked. He said that I was manic-depressive, and told me a little bit about it. The mood swings are the big part—up and down, high and low. You can't really control it.

"That doctor said one thing that, at the time, I thought was sort of mean," Bruce says. "I'm not sure if I understood him right, in fact. He said, 'Bruce, there's just two ways you can go with this disease: You can take this medicine or you can end up jumping off a high bridge.'"

He shakes his head, remembering. "Doesn't that sound funny? I don't know, maybe I just misunderstood. Anyhow, he put me on a drug called lithium, and I've been on that ever since. It kind of balances things out for me when I'm in the manic part of it. It doesn't do anything for the depression part, though."

On the Farm

Has he always had these mood swings? Bruce thinks a moment, and says no.

"I wasn't this way when I was really young," he replies. "I was just like any normal kid. I mean, you can be happy one minute, and maybe sad the next. That's how kids can be, but I wasn't any different than anyone else. I just felt like a regular kid.

"I grew up in a little town not too far from here. We lived on my grandpa's farm; my dad built a house on an acre of land out there. My grandpa had milk cows, but sold them, and we farmed the land—raised oats, soybeans, rye. It was a lot of work, and we all helped. There were six kids in our family—four boys and two girls."

Bruce smiles quietly when asked if being on a farm was a good way to grow up.

"I'll tell you," he says, "some of it was nice. But one of the best memories I have of the farm was waking up early in the morning, before it got light, and hearing rain coming down, running down the gutter outside. That was a good feeling, because it meant that I could sleep in. So I guess that kind of tells you how much I liked all the work on the farm!

Bruce's mood swings prompted him to see a doctor, who prescribed medication.

"My older brother liked it more than I did, I guess. After my grandpa died, though, the land just got rented out to other people. Nobody really wanted to stay on that farm."

NO STUDENT

Bruce didn't like school. He says that he counted the days until he got out.

"We had what they called a modular system back then," he says. "I had all my classes in the morning, and afternoons were free. I guess they did it that way so kids who had jobs or something could arrange their schedules so it worked out. Anyhow, as soon as I turned sixteen, I got a job pumping gas at a gas station in town. They sold bait there, too.

"Now *that* kind of work, I liked. I was real reliable, I'd show up for work on time every day. I liked having money, and I was pretty good about saving it, too. I wanted to buy a car."

He pauses, thinking. "Well, school—you wanted to know about that. I wasn't a bad kid, never sassed the teachers or anything. The only class I liked was woodworking. To this day, I am so mad at myself for waiting until senior year to take it. I really never knew how much I would like it; I took it on a whim, you know, because I needed an extra credit. And it was great.

"I'd go into the woodworking room in the afternoons when there was nothing else going on, and I'd really enjoy being there. I got good at it, too. You know, I even got an award for it, too. It was kind of a combination award for everything I built in there. I got a pin that said it—Craftsman of the Year."

He smiles ruefully. "Man, you know, I wish I still had that pin. I was so proud of it. But I haven't seen it in a very long time."

SENIOR-YEAR PANIC

Bruce says his social life was quiet.

"I was really shy," he explains. "I had very few friends, but I was OK. I hung around with my friend Gordie and my cousin Gale. But when you work, plus you live out on a farm, you don't really have a lot of kids your age around.

"It was during my senior year that I started kind of panicking," he recalls. "Everyone seemed to have a plan for what they were doing after graduation. I knew I wasn't going to college—at least there was one choice I eliminated. The war in Vietnam was just ending, and I wasn't sure what I wanted to do.

"My cousin Gale, he enlisted in the army. And when Gordie decided to go into the navy, I went and took the physical for the navy, too. It wasn't that I wanted to be in the navy, I just was getting panicky, like everyone else knew [what they wanted] and I didn't."

DEPRESSION

That last year of high school was also when Bruce had his first experience with depression.

"Maybe it came from not knowing what I was going to do," he says. "I don't really know. But I remember my days really went by in a flash. I was sleeping a lot, especially during the day, but I'd be up at night. Everything was all mixed up. I told my boss at work I needed time off. My parents knew something was wrong. I wasn't eating, wasn't talking. I went to school and came home— that was it.

"My parents were worried. They took me to the doctor and he put me on medicine to help my depression called Thorazine. But it didn't really work. I was way overmedicated—the stuff made me groggy. It wasn't doing what it was supposed to, either.

"Anyway, that fall after I graduated from high school, I tried to commit suicide," says Bruce, looking embarrassed. "I loaded up a shotgun early in the morning and was getting ready to do it. I was fiddling with the trigger, trying to get the catch off, when my fourteen-year-old sister came into the room. She grabbed the gun away, and that was that."

Does he remember how he felt that morning? Bruce looks sad as he shakes his head.

"I don't," he says. "It was like it happened to somebody else, you know? It's hard to understand, maybe. I wasn't sad. I didn't hear any voices or have any hallucinations. I wasn't anything. I wasn't thinking of anyone else, not thinking at all. I was lost."

TO THE HOSPITAL

After his suicide attempt, Bruce's parents immediately took him to a hospital in a nearby city. They told the doctor what had happened, and he admitted Bruce into the psychiatric ward.

"That was the first hospitalization for me," he says. "And it seems like I've been in and out ever since. It seems like it's been forever.

"They took me off the Thorazine and just kept an eye on me for a while in the hospital. There were groups to go to, sessions where you talked about things [and] visited with other people that had problems. I was there about three weeks, I think. I had a new kind of medicine, and it seemed like I was feeling more like myself. I wasn't so groggy like I was before, anyway. So they let me go home, but as it turned out, I wasn't home for very long."

A nurse takes a sample of Bruce's blood. Bruce sees his doctor regularly to discuss his health and manage his medications.

UNCERTAIN TIMES

Bruce didn't want to stay at home on the farm; he was anxious to be out on his own. He called one of his cousins who lived in the city.

"He told me I could stay with him a while," says Bruce. "So that's what I did. I quit my job at the gas station and moved into the city. I'd get jobs, you know, [but] nothing [for] very long. I'd work for a while, then I'd quit and get another job—just part-time stuff, mostly. I was restless, though. It just seemed like I couldn't settle down with anything.

"I ended up moving out of my cousin's place pretty soon after that. It was too small, really. I'd move in with another friend or a cousin—I don't know. It seemed like there'd be an argument, and it was time to move on, you know? Anyhow, I ended up deciding I wanted to live on my own, so I went to the courthouse in a town to the east of the city. I was trying to find out about housing out there.

"And I was asking about different places, and I guess I got loud and obnoxious. That's what they said, anyway. I don't think I was, but they said not only was I obnoxious but that I threatened to kill someone."

Bruce looks baffled. "I am telling you the truth: I don't ever remember threatening anyone. But what happened? They call the police, and pretty soon I'm being taken to a hospital nearby. They think I'm on drugs or something. This one cop, he says, 'Bruce, what the hell are you on?' He knew my name because he saw it on my license, you know? But I wasn't on anything."

THE STATE HOSPITAL

The authorities kept him in the hospital overnight. Their tests showed that he was not drunk or on drugs.

"But they weren't going to let me go," Bruce explains. "They really thought I was a threat, though. So they put me in a squad car and took me to the state hospital for the mentally ill. It's a huge place. My parents had been contacted, so they knew. I guess everybody thought it was the right thing for me.

"I wasn't committed," he insists. "But I always felt that if I ran away or anything like that, I would get committed. My parents didn't think I should come home, because I guess they figured they really didn't understand what was going on with me. So I did what my parents wanted, and I stayed. And I was there six months. Six months!

"It wasn't a very good place, either," he says. "The upper level was a locked unit. You couldn't get out even if you had to—like if there was a fire or something. It was like a jail. I was in there for a while, a short time. They evaluate you when you're in there, decide if you are dangerous or not."

SOME GOOD PEOPLE

Bruce says that many people at the state hospital would probably be there for the rest of their lives, and that was sad.

"There really are some good people there," he says. "If they could just get some help, they'd get better. The thing is, it's an institution, and it's so big that you could just get forgotten there—just lost. You have no one who cares about you, no one who loves you. You don't get visits, and it seems like no one cares whether you get out or not.

"A lot of the people there have just given up, I think. I tried to get to know some of them. I mean, I was in a lot better shape than they were. One woman was scarred all over, her arms and her face and legs. She had tried to cut herself; she did it on purpose.

Bruce picks up a prescription. The medication helps with his mania, he says, but not with his depression.

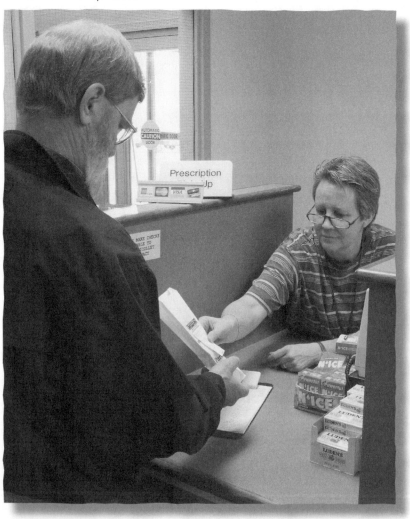

Another older woman jumped out the window. Her brain was damaged so badly when she landed that she has to wear a hockey helmet all the time. She had seizures, too. It was really hard on her.

"Me, I didn't do much. It wasn't like when I was in the other hospital and had lots of therapy sessions. You were pretty much on your own here. One thing that did happen was something I never expected—shock treatments. It was for the depression part of my illness. I took thirteen or fourteen of the treatments, I guess, until the doctors stopped doing it."

He pauses a moment. "They were scary, let me tell you."

"THE BIGGEST NEEDLE YOU EVER SAW"

"Mostly," Bruce admits, "I was afraid of the needle they used each time they gave me a shot. It's a muscle relaxant, and they give it to you right in your hip. It's to calm you down before the shock treatment. Man, that was the biggest needle you ever saw.

"The nurse would tell me to put my arm up in the air, you know, and count backwards starting at ten. Well, you never really get down past three or four, and [then] you're out. So I wasn't awake really. Afterwards, I'd wake up and they told me to sit up and they'd give me breakfast."

Using shock treatments for depression was not uncommon in the state hospital, but Bruce says that he is not entirely sure what the doctors were trying to do.

"They kind of explained it," he says, "but it wasn't very clear to me. I guess it was just a better way of getting to the part of the brain where my trouble was. I don't know, really. I don't think it did anything one way or the other. I didn't feel any different after I'd had all of those treatments. I'm not sure why they stopped. Maybe they figured that nothing was happening, so they just stopped.

"I saw this movie once," Bruce continues, "called *One Flew over the Cuckoo's Nest*. Jack Nicholson was in it, and he had shock treatments, too. He was a sort of troublemaker, I think, and it seemed like they did those treatments to kind of get him in line, like it was a punishment or something. Mine weren't like that. For one thing, I don't think he even had the shots beforehand. And I don't think they were doing mine because they were mad at me, you know?"

21

Bruce received shock treatments in the hospital. "I don't think it did anything one way or the other," he recalls.

"NO"

One day, a staff member at the hospital informed Bruce that he would be leaving soon. He was surprised because he didn't feel that anything had changed since he had arrived.

"I was really shocked, actually," he says. "I remember saying to the doctor, 'I'm not ready to go. I don't know what the hell I'm going to do.' You get in a place for six months, and you start getting used to it. I wanted to leave, I don't mean that I liked it there. But you forget about life outside the hospital. And then, you quick[ly] have to make some plans, like what you're going to do with yourself. Because I was kind of confused about that when I first went in, you know?

"Anyhow, this one staff lady told me that I could go to a care place, kind of like a transition between the state hospital and living on your own. But I said no, because I really wanted to go home. I remember calling and talking to my mother [about going home]. And you know what she said? She said, 'No.' That hurt a lot. She said, 'It's hard for us to do this, but if you came home, we couldn't give you any help. So you aren't coming home, Bruce.'"

Bruce looks down at his hands for a long moment, and then looks back up. "I felt bad, really bad."

LIFE AT THE CARE CENTER

After he was discharged from the hospital, the only option for Bruce was to go to the care center. The center was made up of a number of houses set aside for former patients to live in. There was also a large building where they could get their medications and meals.

"There were a lot of people there," Bruce explains. "Most were pretty easy to get along with. There wasn't much to do there, that was a problem. Lots of sitting around smoking, mostly. But I had a nice roommate, and there were two other guys down the hall I talked to. And the guy who ran the care center, Bob, he was a real nice guy, too.

"I went to him after being there a little while, you know, and I asked him if there was anything I could do to earn a few bucks. I told him I was pretty good with my hands. I was willing to do anything; it would give me something to do during the day. And like I said, I could make some money—for cigarettes, if nothing else. I was getting a social security check each month—like for a disability, you know? I think all of the people there were. But to stay there, you'd sign [the checks] over to the care center, and that would be like your rent money. But you wouldn't have any other money.

"Bob said that I could help shovel snow outside, and he said, 'How about if you mop and clean the hallways of the center, here, and the lobby? And if you want, you can wash dishes.' So I did. I wasn't making a lot of money, but it was nice to feel useful. Besides, I was only nineteen, a lot younger than some of those people. I didn't want to just sit all the time."

"My Life Was New Again"

After working at the center for more than a year, Bruce finally felt as though he was ready to go out on his own.

"Between the hospital and the center, I'd been out of outside life for almost two years," he says. "I'd met a real nice girl named Marge at the center, and we were seeing a lot of each other. She was a resident, too, and she and I were both working in the kitchen. Marge and I decided it was time to go. I wanted a job, you know? I felt like my life was new again.

"What I did was, I took a little walk, just set out one day from the center and walked right down West 7th Street. There was this little hole-in-the-wall gas station. I asked to speak to the manager and told him I wanted a job. It was good timing, because he said he needed someone to pump gas. This was the days before everything was self-service, you know?

"So, I started working the very next day. I stayed at the care center for just a little while, until I got my feet on the ground with the job. When I saved enough, I rented an apartment, and Marge and I were in good shape. I bought a car, too—a blue Pontiac station wagon. It was used, but it ran really good. Things seemed good. We even drove out to see my folks a few times."

Were they pleased to see him? Bruce says he wasn't sure.

"I think my mom was glad to see me," he says. "But with my dad—I don't know if 'pleased' is the right word. It was more like, 'Well, at least Bruce is doing something,' you know what I mean?"

Looking for the Right Job

Bruce had a series of jobs over the next few years. After working at the gas station for two years, he went to work for his cousin Gale, who was home from the army.

"He was managing a 7-Eleven store," says Bruce, "and he hired me on to work behind the counter. I ended up quitting that after a while, though, and I'll tell you why. See, I had medications I was supposed to be taking, and I was being really careful about not missing doses. But Gale changed my shift so I was working nights. See, that's wrong for someone like me, because sleeping in the day and working at night screwed up my medication schedule.

"Plus, there were a lot of punks coming in there all the time," he confides. "They'd shoplift at night, figuring they could get away with it, I guess. Anyway, I finally told Gale I wasn't sleeping enough, and I couldn't do it anymore. I asked for day [shifts], but he said no. So I quit.

"[Then] I had a real good job as a cigarette delivery guy, but it didn't last too long. It wasn't anything against me. I was doing fine. The guy wasn't making enough money, though, so he had to let me go."

Bruce thinks a moment, working out the sequence of events. "Marge and I were married by now," he says. "We wanted to have a baby, but we needed to wait a while, to make sure the money was coming in regularly, you know? That was the key thing—a steady job."

Bruce shares a moment with one of his daughters. His daughters, he says, are "the most important things in my life."

A ROLLER COASTER

But another key thing was Bruce's mental health, and that seemed to be fraying. Even though he was being careful about taking the medication prescribed for his depression, he was having more trouble.

"It seemed like it wasn't just depression anymore," Bruce explains. "I was having problems, talking loud and getting kind of belligerent, I guess you'd say—like I was before I went into the state hospital, when they thought I was on something. It was happening more and more, but then I'd get really depressed, really sad. The medicine helped with some of it, but I was kind of on a roller coaster with my emotions.

"When things got out of hand, I'd end up for a week or two at a hospital, until I could get back to normal. And I always did," he insists. "Sometimes it took a while. Sometimes it was a question of a different medication. And it was about this time when they said that what I had wasn't just depression. It was manic depression, or bipolar, they say now."

"I'D JUST GET IN THE CAR AND GO"

Bruce explains that when he is in the "manic" part of his disease, he is loud and insistent and talks nonstop, often without making any sense.

"I'd be up all hours," he says. "I'd be fidgeting, you know, and Marge was kind of in between being scared at what was wrong with me or angry. So I'd just get in the car and go—no destination in mind, usually. Like this one time, I was driving home from work, and I was really manic, really on a euphoric high. And I was imagining things happening that really weren't.

"That's the thing—they're not hallucinations because I'm not seeing things that aren't there. I just interpret them differently. Like when I was driving home from work, I was speeding. A police car started to pull me over, but I decided I couldn't stop. I kept going faster and faster. Well, the cop wasn't going to give up. The thing turned into a big high-speed chase, with other troopers and cops following me, surrounding me.

"They finally swerve in front, kind of trapping me, and I had to stop. They got out with their guns drawn. They dragged me out of my car, and they were *mad*. The one says, 'What the hell do you think you're doing?' And I told them the truth: I was worried about the Second Coming of Jesus, and I had to get home. I was scared, and I really thought that it was happening."

"THAT'S NOT ME!"

Bruce is still amazed that he made a statement like that.

"I go to church, sure," he says, shaking his head in disbelief. "But if you know me, you'd say that I'd never come up with that. I don't talk like that. I mean, that's not me! I'm not a supereligious person who thinks about the Second Coming. But in my manic phases, I guess I do."

The police were at a loss to explain his behavior. He didn't appear to be intoxicated. They took him to jail, and he later appeared before a judge.

"I think somehow they had gotten ahold of my dad," says Bruce. "I can't really remember how it all happened, but anyway, he must have told them that I had problems. So, the judge sent me to the psychiatric ward at a hospital in town and told me that when I got better, I could do my punishment. It was two hundred hours of community service; I did lots of jobs at a center for people with heart problems, I think.

"But anyway, that was pretty much how things were going. I'd start a job, then I'd have problems and end up in the hospital again for a while, then I'd get out. Then we had a baby—Pam, she's my oldest—and another daughter, Jessie. But instead of having a great family life, mine was coming apart."

"THE GIRLS GOT REALLY SCARED"

Bruce says he has no one to blame but himself for the misery he put his family through.

"We were living in a trailer park at the time," he says. "The girls were really little, and I was having more and more problems. And I want to make it really clear—I was never violent, I never hit Marge or the girls, or threatened them. But I yelled."

He shakes his head sadly. "I really yelled a lot," he admits. "Sometimes I'd go into big lectures about religion, about how the world was ending and Jesus was coming again. And I yelled about money, too. I think I was working in an office, in the mail room doing shipping and receiving at the time. I was making money, but it never seemed like enough. I don't know. I would get really anxious, and then I'd go into my manic thing, yelling about how we

Bruce enjoys a close relationship with his daughters but admits that his behavior scared his daughters when they were younger.

are broke, how we're going to lose our home. I'd turn on the radio really loud, too, really blast the music. I'm not sure why.

"[My wife would] argue with me, try to get me straight. She was working part-time, but mostly she was staying home with the girls. But anyway, at night when I'd be talking a hundred miles an hour, yelling and ranting, I remember the girls got really scared. There was this little cabinet in the trailer, and they'd climb in there to hide when I got loud. They'd cry and hide. At the time, I didn't even notice. And after a while, I'd get done yelling and I'd do what I always did—I'd get in the car and drive."

"HE TOLD HER THAT I REALLY NEEDED SOME HELP"

On one occasion, Bruce pointed the car north and drove until he ran out of gas. Still manic, he walked for hours in the dark, not really sure where he was headed.

"I didn't know where I was going, why I was going," he says. "I was just going. I started hitchhiking, and a guy picked me up. I fell asleep when I got in his truck. I think I was exhausted. That's sometimes what happens when the euphoria goes away, I crash. But anyway, he let me off after a while and I kept walking.

"I ended up at a farmer's place, way out in the country. I was so hungry, and I asked him for a piece of bread or something. He was nice; he let me come in and he fed me ham sandwiches and milk. Then off I went, walking, walking, until I came to some little town. A lady starts calling me, 'Bruce! Bruce!' I don't recognize her, but it turns out she's a friend of one of my sisters. It was a real coincidence, you know?

"Anyhow, she tells me to come home with her. I think she realizes I'm not really sure of myself. So, she and her husband Dave let me stay the night, and then in the morning he takes me back home to Marge and the trailer. I went inside, and he talked to Marge. I think he told her that I really needed some help. So after he left, Marge and a neighbor drove me to the hospital again."

He laughs humorlessly. "Again."

THE TOUGHEST PART

Bruce stayed at the hospital for a while, and then was transferred to another state hospital.

"I think it was because my insurance had run out," he admits. "Those hospital stays get expensive, especially the ones that go for weeks, or even months. I can remember being in the hospital, the doctors doing tests on me, and it seemed like I'd never get out. I missed Marge and the girls so much.

"I felt so bad," he says, his voice catching. "I felt like I'd let them down. I was in a locked unit for a long time, and then later got moved to a cottage, where I was only locked in at night. One time—I'll never forget it—I was in the hospital, feeling bad, and all of a sudden I hear this little voice yell 'Daddy!' And here this little tiny kid was running down the hall to see me! It was Jessie—my youngest girl. My dad had come to visit and had brought her along. What a lift that gave me.

"But you know what the toughest part about being in the hospital is? It's getting out, coming home. Hard to believe, but it's true. You come home and you got a page of instructions, all these new medications, the dose, the time you need to take them. And it feels like you just can't quite get your feet on the ground. It seems like it's taking forever, you know? Just trying to get back to normal, only it's so hard."

THE RIGHT MEDICINE

Bruce and Marge divorced soon after his stay in the state hospital, although they have tried to remain friends.

"I don't blame her one bit," he says. "I was terrible to live with. But anyway, after that, she and the girls moved out of the trailer, and I couldn't afford it anymore, anyway. The bank got the trailer, and I moved in here, to this apartment. I've been here ever since, and my girls are grown up now. Pam's twenty now, and Jessie's sixteen.

"That last hospital stay I was telling you about, they put me on not only antidepressant medication but something that keeps me from having the manic stuff. It's an antipsychotic drug. And that's helped a lot. In fact, since then, I've only had one episode.

"That was several years ago, too. I started driving again, same as before," he says. "It's hard to remember what you were thinking when you're manic, you know? It's like you're not really yourself. I

Bruce hopes to someday leave his cleaning job and pursue woodworking or some other more enjoyable work.

was going to Washington, D.C., I think, but I'm not sure why. I got car trouble about three hundred miles from home, and ended up coming home.

"I was still really manic, and I cranked up the TV and the stereo loud. I was hearing messages in the lyrics of the music—I was psychotic. And of course, the police show up, the neighbors have complained, I guess. Anyhow, I was getting wound up into the Second Coming again and not making any sense. And so it was the same deal. This time, my brother came over and got me back into the hospital. They got me on different medication, got me calmed down.

"But I really was worried that time because I'd been taking my medications. I asked the doctor what happened. I guess I had believed that as long as I remembered to take everything I was supposed to, I'd be OK. But he just said, 'Bruce, we just don't know.' Just like that. So I guess I have to just be more aware of the signs that maybe I'm getting manic—that's how it starts. And maybe I can head it off before it turns into another trip to the hospital."

"What I Wish"

Bruce says that he doesn't get mad about too much, but he does resent the way bipolar disorder has affected his life.

"Like my job," he says. "I told you how you have to kind of ease back into things after being in the hospital, take it easy a little. But it feels like it's taking forever. Now I'm working for a temporary service, doing cleaning at the mall. That's my job."

He shakes his head, looking as though he is fighting tears. "Man, you don't strain your brain doing that, cleaning the floors and scraping gum off the benches," he says sarcastically. "No pressure. I guess that's what I have to have—jobs with no pressure. But I resent it. I don't want to be doing this all my life. My girls—they insist they're not ashamed of me, but I'm ashamed of myself. I feel like I've let everybody down, including me.

"What I wish is that I could afford a little house somewhere— get away from this damned apartment complex. You know what I'd do? I'd make up a workroom, get some tools. Man, I haven't done carpentry in a while. That was always the one thing I was really good at."

He smiles and shrugs. "Maybe it could happen," he says.

Mike

"I CAN'T HAVE FRIENDSHIPS WITH REGULAR PEOPLE. MEN, WOMEN, IT DOESN'T MATTER. I JUST DON'T SEEM TO INTERACT WITH THEM."

The man seems nervous as he gets into the car. He is flushed and a bit out of breath. "I'm late," he announces, a little too loudly. "I got talking to a guy at the bus stop, and I guess we just weren't really thinking about the time. Anyway," he says, shrugging, "I'm Mike. You wanted to talk to me?"

Mike is forty but looks younger. He's dark, with glasses that give his face a square, solid look. Sitting in the front seat of the car, he seems to be more and more uncomfortable. He sits very close to the car door, as if he might need to get out quickly. He clears his throat several times. He drums his fingers on the dashboard and hums to himself. Clearly unhappy in the confined space of the car, Mike is visibly relieved when we reach our destination—a small branch library in the heart of the city.

"THEY THINK THEY'RE PRETTY SMART"

"Oh yeah," he says, walking up to the doors. "I recognize this place. I guess I've seen all the libraries in the city. I ride my bike a lot, and I've been pretty much everywhere. I don't think there's a neighborhood or a part of the city I haven't ridden through at some time or another."

Mike has been diagnosed with something called schizotypal personality disorder. He seems uncertain as to what that means, but he knows that psychiatrists have told him that he is paranoid. He has experienced feelings of being persecuted and has had psychotic episodes, in which his understanding of reality is skewed.

32

His troubles have been compounded by his substance abuse, especially alcohol. Talking with Mike, it is easy to see that he feels that other people are singling him out, hurting him on purpose. Those intense feelings are a part of schizotypal disorder.

"I'll tell you," he says, settling into his chair in one of the library's interview rooms. "Those guys, those psychiatrists? They are jerks. I mean, half of them get into the field because they are nuts themselves, you know? And they think they're pretty smart when they come up with a diagnosis after one visit with you. I don't trust them, not at all," he says, shaking his head.

"I've been on medication for years, two different things that the psychiatrists have prescribed. But I got sick of it. I'm not taking the stuff anymore. I just saw my psychiatrist today, in fact. I told him, no more."

What was the doctor's reaction? Mike shrugs and looks away for an instant. "He thought it was a good idea. He said, 'Go for it, give it a try.'" Mike starts drumming his fingers on the table and meets my eyes, as if to say, "Hey, believe it or not—it's up to you."

Mike has schizotypal personality disorder, an illness that makes it difficult for him to have relationships with other people.

The Marine

Mike acknowledges that it was during his time in the marines that he was first diagnosed with mental illness.

"I was on active duty there," he says. "I was nineteen when I enlisted. And really, to tell the truth, I really hated it. It was all about rules, obeying someone else's orders, following along like sheep. Very different than I thought it would be."

But why was that a surprise? Didn't he know that branches of the military are all based on obeying orders? Mike smiles and shrugs.

"To some extent, maybe," he replies. "But it was really a very different experience for me. I think the social setting was weird, and I had a hard time with it. See, I figured that the marines was like this noble cause, with a proud tradition, right? And I figured that I'd be around people that were good, who wanted to do something good for their country—positive, I guess."

He shakes his head in disgust. "But I saw a lot of really degenerate people. Everybody was on drugs, everybody drank. Everywhere you looked, people were on something—mostly pot, heroin. And it really bothered me. I was disillusioned."

Fitting In

Mike says that to fit in, he began using drugs and drinking, too. He admits that he had smoked pot a little when he was younger, but insisted it was meaningless.

"Just like when you're fourteen," he explains. "I don't even think I liked it back then. But in the marines, it was different. And if you didn't use, you weren't one of them. So I guess I was afraid of not fitting in; I didn't want to be on the outside, like in high school. So I went along.

"Yeah, I got caught a couple of times. See, they'd do what are called UAs—that's where they check your urine to see if you're using [drugs]. You couldn't get away with it. Traces would show up, so you would be busted."

Mike says that only certain people were tested and that he was viewed with suspicion by some of the commanding officers. Because they didn't like or trust him, he says, he was tested more often than others.

"Yeah, the officers were pretty down on me," he explains. "I'd had a couple of Article 15s; in the civilian world, that's like going

Mike was first diagnosed with a mental illness while he was a teenager serving in the Marine Corps.

to court. You go in front of a commanding officer, and he pretty much decides your fate. My first Article 15 was disrespecting a NCO [noncommissioned officer]. But really, the guy was way out of line. He actually should have been given the Article 15, not me."

Mike says that he had gotten into a shouting match with the NCO, a sergeant of the guard, a man who had it in for him.

"I was coming off a shift. I was stationed up in the Aleutian Islands. We were seven hundred miles from Siberia, and my job was to guard nuclear weapons. So anyway, I was tired after my shift and thinking about going back to the base, and this sergeant came up screaming at me. I had no idea what was the matter. And he put his arms up like he was going to take a swing at me, and I punched him.

"I figured I'd better defend myself, right? I mean, that was like a reflex, an automatic thing to do. And the next thing I know, I'm being charged with disrespect. I know the guy was pretty much setting me up—he hated me. See, he knew me from this bar we had on base—we called it the Tundra Tavern. The sergeant's wife came in there a lot. She was really a lush. And ugly as sin, but she had a nice body," he adds, laughing.

"What Did I Get Myself Into?"

"So one night," he continues, "I guess I kind of put my hand on her butt. Just the one time. And I guess it got back to him, and he was really mad. He told me that he would get me someday. That's just how he said it, too.

"I was really angry after I appeared for my Article 15. I mean, here's this dirty little piece of humanity, this sergeant, lying to the commanding officer. So I got docked a couple of months' pay, and got broken down to private. I'd been a private first class. So, big deal.

Looking back on his early discharge from the marines, Mike says, "I was glad to be rid of them."

"The second Article 15 was when some guys and I went out on a nice 60-degree day, hiking around with a backpack full of beer. We sort of broke into this cabin and spent the afternoon in there. It had been abandoned, and we didn't steal anything. Actually, the officers who caught us accused us of writing satanic stuff on the walls. But we didn't. It was there when we arrived," he says.

"Anyway, [that was] another Article 15 for me," he sighs, remembering. "I knew I'd made a mistake joining the marines. Truthfully? I guess I knew I'd made a mistake the first night I was there. I remember lying in bed, saying to myself, 'What did I get myself into?' I felt like I was in this cage of dirty, immoral hooligans. I mean, they were just barely held together by the rules they had. They were awful, and the officers weren't any better. Actually, they were a bunch of idiots."

"Something Not Quite Right"

Asked whether he thought that he was at all responsible for any of the trouble he got into, Mike flushes, visibly offended.

"No," he says, through clenched teeth. "I was actually being reasonable, which they *weren't*. I mean, I made the conscious decision not to let them tell me what to do. Especially when it was something stupid, like get up at five in the morning to go running in a damned blizzard. I'm not kidding, that's what we did.

"So when five A.M. came, and we were supposed to appear at formation, I just rolled over and went back to sleep. I said, 'To hell with this.' Other guys went out, I stayed. And pretty soon, the commanding officer is standing there by my cot and I look up at him. And you know what I did then?"

He smirks. "I rolled over again and went back to sleep! Seriously, nobody is going to tell me what to do, when to do it, none of that. That's it. And so they decide there's something not quite right, you know? Like in my thinking. So I go see the shrink, and we talk, had this little interview. No big deal. The end result was that I got what's called an expeditious discharge—I was out in twenty-one months. I had signed on for four years. I guess they were glad to get rid of me, like I was glad to be rid of them."

High School Horrors

Mike's voice has gotten very loud in the last few minutes, and he is leaning far forward in his chair. He seems unaware of the fact that he is almost shouting. He crosses and uncrosses his legs, and settles back.

"I have to tell you, I didn't finish high school. I mean, that's why I joined the marines, to get out of high school. It was a horror, I'm telling you. I was a nervous wreck every morning just thinking about going to school. It wasn't so much the work, it was just the social stuff, you know? And the teachers were pretty stupid.

"This one teacher, she had a Czech last name, and it was pretty hard to pronounce. It started with a *SJ*, but the *S* was silent. Anyway, the whole year I had her, she completely butchered my name. I mean, I know it's tricky, because it's Polish, but jeez—you'd think she'd be a little more sensitive to that, wouldn't you? I always had the feeling, you know, that she was doing it deliberately. Anyway, I hated her class, mostly because of her."

"NOWADAYS, YOU'D GET ARRESTED"

He smiles. "I brought these two Civil War pistols to class one day— they were cap and ball revolvers. I think we'd been talking about the Civil War or something, I don't remember. But as I was standing up in front of the class, I thought about how funny it would have been if I'd loaded them up. I really considered it—not shooting at anybody, of course not, but just shooting out the lights in the room. That would have been something, just to see her face, just to get her reaction. I would have gotten a big bang out of that. I mean, hell, it was fun seeing a couple of the kids get scared when I took them out of my coat!"

Mike acknowledges that he got a real feeling of power that day in ninth grade. "My teacher didn't get mad that I brought the [guns] in. I mean, nowadays, you'd get arrested, right? I can see that it's a different situation now, since kids have gotten shot and everything.

"But in another way, the cops tend to really overreact these days. I mean, I've had guns pointed at me for doing nothing—nothing! These stupid local cops, they overreact like crazy. I mean, one day I'm standing in my doorway—I was talking to the cops—and I wasn't doing anything wrong. I was making no sudden movements, not gesturing with my hands, nothing. All of a sudden, the one cop whips out his gun and points it at me and says, 'Let me see your left hand.' I had no idea what he was talking about. I was scared, sure. It's just weird, these guys don't have proper training, I guess."

Asked about why the police had come to his door, Mike shakes his head. He doesn't feel like talking about it right now, he says, but maybe he will later.

Mike recalls his feelings of being singled out and treated unfairly while in high school.

"I JUST STARTED HITTING HIM"

Mike admits that he was not well liked in high school, and he thinks that maybe the beginnings of his mental illness started there. He didn't just *imagine* that he was being persecuted, he says; he *was* singled out.

"Mostly it was the jocks. I was always getting beat up, or being threatened with getting beat up. Really, like I said, the constant anxiety about getting in fights was really hard on me. It was like a sensation overload—I was on edge all the time. A lot of kids didn't like me. And no," he says, glaring, "I *don't* know why.

"It wasn't like I was a shrimp or anything. I was medium build, medium height. But these jocks in our school, they'd just go after me. This one guy, this big slob, he was 250 pounds, like twice my size. And he was nothing but a big overbearing bully. But he was a baby, too. This one time I was standing in the lunch line, and he came by. I knew he was going to start up with me; I could just sense it.

"So I just started hitting him, bam, bam, bam. I thought, 'I'm not taking any more of this crap.' Well, he got in such an emotional state over that, he turned beet red, like he was going to cry. He waited until I wasn't looking, and he hit me in the back of the neck. Boy, I've never been hit that hard, ever. I was knocked out, and he got in trouble. He deserved it."

REACTIONS

Did he have any friends? A girlfriend? Mike shakes his head absentmindedly. No, he really didn't.

"I did have this one guy, Ron, that I hung out with sometimes. I'd known him since grade school. No one else was interested in spending time with him, either, so I guess we sort of had each other—kind of like by default. Ron was really weird. A one-track mind, that was Ron. All he thought about was cars. I'd say, 'Ron, you want to go to a movie?' And he'd say, 'No, I'm gonna work on my car.' Or 'Hey Ron, you want to cruise around downtown, look for girls?' And he'd say, 'No, I'm gonna work on my car.'

"Just a weirdo," Mike laughs. "I've never been into cars that much, so I'd just pretend I was. But I didn't care much about what he was talking about. So maybe he was classified as a friend then, but not really. We were just the two rejects, you know?"

Mike says that, in general, he was pretty quiet in school, but he made plans sometimes, schemes that he could carry out to get a reaction.

"Like I'd have some fun—just on my own, you know? Not with Ron or anything. I'd go in the bathroom [and] take some M-80s. I'd make a fuse out of toilet paper, twist it up really good, long enough so that I'd have time to get out of there before the explosion. And then I attached the M-80 to the fuse and lit it. Man!" he says, smiling. "I could sometimes get halfway up the stairs before it went off. Nobody ever knew it was me. Just shaking things up. Just kid stuff."

OUT OF THE HOUSE

But as much as Mike hated high school, he says, becoming a marine was no better. And having been discharged two years before his term of enlistment was over—even though it was what he wanted—he felt ashamed coming home.

"My parents didn't really say much about it," he says. "My dad did say once that growing up being picked on at school and stuff, he was surprised that I put up with the marines as long as I did. You know, getting screamed at by the officers, stuff like that. But I still felt ashamed.

"I lived at home for a few months, just to get back on my feet. I was paying my own way, paying rent. I didn't want to freeload. But

I was still smoking pot [and] drinking. I had a job, but I was using a lot of my money buying marijuana and stuff. I guess I'd gotten into a bad habit in the service. Well, my dad got mad one night. We really got in a fight. He said something, I said something. We started pushing each other, and he yells at me, 'I quit liking you a long time ago!' Wham—that really hurt. I never did forget that. He apologized right away, said he didn't mean it. But I know he did."

The next day, Mike moved out of his parents' home. He was offered a space in a trailer with some people he knew.

"I wouldn't call them friends," he says, his voice getting louder. "They were trailer trash. It was Ron's sister, and her boyfriend, and another girl. And it was a real party house, they were drinking and smoking every night, really late. And I had a job. I was supposed to be getting up early every morning. I'd be lying in bed, and the music would be so loud, and I could hear them saying, 'What's with him, why does he go to bed so early?' They were clueless. I'm thinking, 'Hey, geniuses, I have to be up at five to go to work. Work, as in a job—not like you guys who do nothing.'"

BETRAYED

Although he wasn't fond of his roommates, Mike says that he tried to be friendly. But they—along with his friend Ron—betrayed him, and that he has never been able to forgive.

"It started one night," he says. "We were sitting around just talking about things—Ron was there, too. And the name of this one cop came up. Nobody liked him; he lived out near where we were. He was one of those guys who loves to hassle people over stuff that wasn't even very important. We sort of all agreed that we hated him.

"So, I said, 'Well, how about if I make some Molotov cocktails (they're like firebombs) and we could put them under his car some night?' I wasn't going to really do it, of course. It was just a kind of bragging, you know. It's just having something to say, trying to be one of the group. But they all thought it sounded like a great idea. We made a bunch of them and just took them outside and threw them around—nothing ever became of it.

"But anyway, the next thing I know, a couple of days later, here come some cops after me, including the one we had been talking about. They accuse me of making terroristic threats against him, saying that I was planning to go after this cop, burn his house down. They said I was going to hurt his kid, too!"

After trying unsuccessfully to live with roommates, Mike now lives alone.

He shakes his head incredulously. "I mean, can you imagine? I'm thinking, how did this get back to the cop, and why was it all of a sudden my idea? And most of all, how did it all get exaggerated like this? And the answer had to be Ron, his sister, the friend. They all got together and shanghaied me—betrayed me, sold me out."

STATE HOSPITAL

The police took Mike to jail, and after talking to a number of people, he was transferred to the state hospital.

"They thought I was nuts," he laughs bitterly. "They were just like the marines; they thought I was having some kind of a mental

42

illness deal going on. I was taken to the state hospital for a mental health evaluation, to see what was the matter.

"Of course, nobody wondered why my supposed friends would make up stories about me wanting to go after a cop, things that I didn't even say. Nope, it was just a question of me having something going on upstairs in my head that other people didn't have. So I went there and stayed for sixty days. I got evaluated, and after it was all done, they threw a lot of words at me.

"Schizophrenia, schizotypal personality, paranoid, disordered personality—you name it, I seemed to have it," he says. "I mean, I will admit that sometimes I have paranoid tendencies; I feel like people are persecuting me. But schizophrenic? I don't buy it. I mean, schizos hear voices, don't they? I don't hear voices, I don't hallucinate."

Mike does admit that there are blank spots in his memory, especially about stressful times. "I think it was when I got to the state hospital that I really found out what happened to me, how I got there. Man, I don't even remember too much about the jail. I think they ended up dropping the charges, but I couldn't swear to it. I do remember calling Ron from the hospital, but he didn't want to take my calls. He didn't want anything to do with me. So that's how I figured that they all set me up."

He takes off his glasses and rubs his eyes. "I need a break," he says.

THE WORST PART OF HAVING MENTAL ILLNESS

Mike spends a little while looking around in the library, inspecting the books on the shelves. When he sits down again, he seems calmer, more introspective.

"I was thinking, you know, about being mentally ill," he says. "I don't know if there's a name for what I've got. I don't know if the psychiatrists in the marines and at the state hospital and all the other ones I've seen know anything. Maybe they're right, maybe they aren't. But the thing I know? I know that I can't interact with normal people.

"I can't have friendships with regular people. Men, women, it doesn't matter. I just don't seem to interact with them. My life always takes me places with the fringe groups, like Ron and his sister and people who are—I don't know—weird, I guess. Some are bad people, some are immoral or amoral, some are people who don't care about anyone but themselves. I guess some of them are like me, but I'm not sure I've met anyone like that.

"It's bad luck, really. I end up in the service with people who drink and do drugs. I end up in apartments with people who do drugs and get me doing them, too. Total degenerates. They tend to be bad people. That's the absolute worst thing about having mental illness. Like I said, that's why I ended up with someone like Ron for a friend in high school—he was a fringe guy, a loser. No one wanted to be his friend but me, because I was desperate."

"DRINK, DRINK, DRINK"

Mike says that after getting out of the hospital, he ended up renting an apartment—another bad experience with fringe people, he says.

"They were all drinkers," he remembers. "I tried to be friendly with them. At first, it seemed like things were OK. But they talked behind your back. They acted nice to your face, and then as soon as you'd walk away, they'd be cutting you down. It wasn't just me that noticed it, either. I was so stressed from living in that building that I started drinking.

"Really," he insists, "I'd wake up in the morning and I'd be so anxiety-ridden, I'd head for the bar. Drink, drink, drink—that was me. And yeah, I got out of control a few times. I'd get going on these ten-day benders, you know, and I'd be out of control. The police showed up a few times, yeah."

But surely he doesn't blame the people in the apartment building for his drinking rampages, especially since they weren't with him when he was drinking, does he? Mike looks annoyed, as though he is tired of explaining it.

"BACK OFF!"

"I had to get out of there," he says with exaggerated slowness. "I had to be somewhere else, where people weren't so bad all the time. But the apartment manager, he was friends with all these people, and he'd take their side. He'd tell me, 'You stay in your apartment; don't be knocking on anyone's door.' But I went up to this one girl's apartment to use her phone. I wasn't on real bad terms with her—she was pretty nice. But someone saw me knock on her door and called the manager."

He scowls. "See what I mean? They were just waiting for me to break the rules, knock on a door. But I knew what was going to happen, I was ready for it. I knew the stupid manager would call the cops. And that's just what he did."

Mike says that he did not want a scene with the police at his door, but he vowed that he was not going to be arrested for something he didn't do.

"I barricaded myself in," he says, his voice getting louder. "I'm telling you, I was not going to let them push me around. I'm sick of it!"

His face is flushed, and he seems momentarily confused, unsure of whether he is talking about the present or the past. His eyes fill

Because of his disorder, Mike's transportation options are limited. He gets around town by bus, bicycle, or on foot.

with tears. "I'm serious," he says. "They have no goddamn right to come in my door, and they can just back off. *Back off!* I told them they were harassing me, and it was against the law. I didn't do anything wrong or illegal."

Mike's voice quavers. "They tried tricking me—having someone down the hall come to my door and try to convince me to open it. But I'm not stupid. I'm not falling for their stupid traps, you know? Because who knows what the cops would have done if I'd opened the door? Were they going to arrest me? Beat me up? Put me in the state hospital again? No way.

"No f———way," he says. "Pardon my French."

MORE RUN-INS

That particular incident ended with the police leaving, Mike says. They had not been able to force him to open his door, so they gave up. But it was not the last time Mike would have dealings with the police.

"I had been drinking in this one bar one night," he admits. "I mean, it was really the drinking that was the problem. I'd had just a few, you know. And—I don't know—they said that I punched out the glass from the door of the bar. I don't remember it to tell you the truth. Or maybe it's a vague memory. But I do have scars."

He holds up one battered hand. "I don't remember any glass breaking. But the bar called the police, and when they took me to jail, they told me that people had surrounded me after I broke the glass. Again, no memory of that. But I do remember the thirty-six hours I spent in jail. It was hellish because I was coming off this medication. That's the important thing, see, it's the medication that makes me so anxious."

A DIFFERENT REALITY

Mike says that one of the medications he has been on has been very difficult for him, and he believes that it accounts for both his drinking and his anxiety.

"I'll admit I'm partly to blame," he says, smiling. "I don't manage medications very well all the time. Anyway, I get the prescriptions for the medications from my psychiatrist, and I make the appointments with him way in advance. But I was sometimes taking more than I should of this one medication—Klonopin. It's kind of addictive, I guess.

Remembering to take his medications and keep his prescriptions filled are daily challenges for Mike.

"And so anyway, I'd run out of Klonopin early, since I took too much. And I'd have like a week or more before my psychiatrist appointment, and I'd be out of the medication that I really needed. That one, Klonopin, is for when someone has really bad anxiety. So I would be out of the Klonopin, and I'd be really having trouble with bad anxiety. It's hard to describe it to someone if you've never felt it.

"I'd be on a bus, you know? And I was just in complete sensory overload, like everything was too much, too loud, too visual, too everything. Like all the sights and sounds are magnified times a thousand. A little noise would sound like an explosion. And, naturally, I was terrified. I mean, who wouldn't be? Just terrified, to the extent that I couldn't even walk. I was so overwhelmed with fear that I couldn't walk to get off the bus. And it wasn't just that I *felt* terrified, it was obvious to other people, too. You'd spot me right away.

"I remember one guy came up to me during one of these times and asked me if I was OK. I was so tense that I was walking really rigid, like I couldn't bend anything. And some guy in a car honks, and I really almost had a heart attack. I thought I'd pass out, right there in the street. Anyway, that's what it's like when I'm coming off the medication, when I can't make it to my next appointment. So then, I'd drink, just to calm down. And drink some more, and before you knew it, I'd be in trouble again."

GETTING OFF MEDICATION

Mike's other medication was an antipsychotic that is designed to help the disordered thinking that schizotypal people have, the kind of thinking that often becomes paranoid.

"I get these ideas that aren't right," he says. "Disordered thinking, they call it. But the drug I was on for that, I didn't like. I'm

Everyday activities are difficult for Mike when he is off his medication.

supposed to take it at night, but it really speeds up your heartbeat. I'm talking 130, 140 beats per minute—lying in bed! I'd be trying to get to sleep, and my heart would be going a mile a minute. I got scared, thought I was having a heart attack then, too. It's like I can't win, you know?

"So I saw the psychiatrist yesterday. I told him I've stopped taking both the medications. He asked me how I was functioning, and I told him about the same as when I was on the medications. I mean, I'm not saying I'm cured. But why take that stuff if it isn't doing any good? I was still paranoid, according to other people, and so if I'm on it or not, what's the difference?"

What about higher doses of the medications? Would it help his paranoia to have more of the drug in his system? He shakes his head.

"I've been on more, been on less," he says. "Doesn't do any good for me. It takes away a lot of your motor skills, like it's hard to respond or react quickly. That's no good for someone like me who rides a bike all the time. It also distorts your perception of time. Like this one time, when I got hit by a car when I was on my bike, the nurse asked me when the accident happened. And I couldn't tell her. Was it yesterday? Last week? A month ago? God, that scared me. It must be like having Alzheimer's or something."

MIKE'S THEORY

Mike says that he told his psychiatrist that he was going to try a new plan without the chemicals.

"I'm just going to find good things to concentrate on," he says. "Maybe start eating right, exercising. I asked him if that would help, and he thought it might. I guess the thing he just wants to know is whether I'm functioning OK. Like, I'm not using my hand to punch out windows or something.

"The thing is," he says, "I've spent most of my adult life *without* medication. So, I can do it."

But hasn't he also spent most of his adult life in trouble and acting inappropriately? He shrugs.

"Yeah, maybe, but the older I get," he says, "the more I look around and say, 'Who really cares?' I mean, so what if people don't understand me or like me? I frankly don't want to associate with most of them. It's not important. It is, sure, when you're in high school, because nobody wants to be on the outside when everyone else is inside. But now? Not an issue for me.

49

"I don't have a girlfriend, don't really have a friend right now. But I guess I like being alone more than trying to fit in with people. I have things that I can do on my own, that I enjoy doing. I ride my bike—I already told you that. And in the winter I hike around. I take buses sometimes, but mostly walk."

Mike looks around, as though he has forgotten something. He spots his backpack on the floor under his chair and puts it on the table. He carefully pulls out a sketch pad with pencil drawings of wildlife—raccoons, skunks, and wildcats.

"I wanted to show you something," he says, his voice a little more gentle. "This is one thing I've been doing lately. Most of these I copied from magazines or books. I didn't trace them—just copied. I really like animals. I guess you can tell, right?"

He turns the pages of the sketch pad slowly, past a very realistic drawing of a cat. He smiles.

"We had a lot of pets, living out in the country—dogs, puppies, kittens, rabbits. We found these orphan skunks one day, down by our woodpile. They were obviously orphaned, you know? Maybe the mom went off and left them, or got hit by a car or something. But they were totally on their own, tiny little things. We started taking care of them, leaving saucers of milk, stuff like that. They stayed around.

"Anyway, I am working on one of these pictures to give my mom for Mother's Day. She'll like it."

Has he considered taking an art class? He closes the sketch pad abruptly, his face getting a closed look. The mood has obviously been broken.

"No," he says. "I want to teach myself. The last thing I want is somebody pointing out things I'm doing wrong, criticizing me. I'm learning plenty just doing it on my own. I've already figured out some stuff about shading, texture, stuff like that."

Trying Not to Think About the Future

What does Mike think about his own future? Is it something he enjoys thinking about, or is that sort of daydreaming stressful for someone with schizotypal behavior?

"I'll tell you a goal," he says, his voice still clipped. "I'd like eventually to come to a point where I don't think about stuff like that, stuff like whether I'll get married or where I'll live or what kind of job I'll have. I have a job now—not a great one, but I get paid. It's doing odd jobs for people, shoveling snow, stuff like that.

Mike enjoys drawing animals. "I am working on one of these pictures to give my mom for Mother's Day," he says.

In the summer I mow lawns. I don't have much stress in that job, so I don't know if I want to change to another kind of work.

"I know it isn't the kind of life my parents thought I'd have. But I can't live up to what everyone else wants. My parents are great, though. They don't act disappointed in me. They might be, underneath, but they don't say anything. They'd like to see me in a normal life, a normal job. But I don't see it happening for me."

He thinks a moment. "I admit I envy people who have friends who care about them," he says. "I already told you I don't have friends right now. It would be fun to have someone that likes the same stuff I do. I've never had anyone like that. So maybe that would be a goal."

He picks up the sketch pad, puts it back into his backpack, and adjusts his hat. It's clearly time to go.

Joann

"IT WAS AS IF MY MIND WAS MISFIRING, SO I COULDN'T THINK STRAIGHT. THE THOUGHTS WERE FLYING SO FAST . . . AND THAT WAS BOTH FRIGHTENING AND EXHAUSTING."

Joann isn't sure she wants to be interviewed. She hasn't talked to many people about the bouts of psychotic behavior that, on several occasions, alarmed her family so much that they brought her to the hospital. Her therapist knows, of course, and her family. She also told a trusted friend or two.

Joann is an attractive woman with an athletic build, a mother of three, and a nurse practitioner with many responsibilities. She hasn't eaten lunch yet, even though it's almost two o'clock. She pulls out a container of potato salad and a plate of salmon from the refrigerator and offers to share.

ATYPICAL DEPRESSION

Joann lives with her husband, Joseph, and their three children in an older home in the city, which is well maintained, with oak floors and comfortable furniture. Colorful Native American relics—some framed, some inside a glass table—are displayed throughout the living room.

"This part out here," she says, smiling and separating a slice of salmon, "this is the clean part of the house. But most of my personal space—my desk and things like that—that's really cluttered. Maybe that's the way it is in most houses, I don't know. I know I'm a real pack rat. I collect things and it's very hard to part with them later on.

"Anyway, I've got a brain disorder, mental illness. I don't know, the word *mental* has all sorts of weird connotations, you know? Like when people say that someone is acting mental, it sounds awful. What I have is called atypical depression. The 'atypical' part means that it is not like ordinary clinical depression. It took a while for the doctors to diagnose, too. I've had episodes of psychosis, where I've had a hard time with what is real and what isn't.

"Depression by itself is an illness that seems to be more understood. People tend to get what it means when someone has clinical depression. But a person who sees things or interprets them in an

Joann has been diagnosed with atypical depression. She has experienced vivid hallucinations and deep depression.

abnormal way—that isn't understood. I guess that's why I've been reluctant to talk much about my disorder. I know it can make people feel uncomfortable."

An Active Childhood

Did her childhood seem to indicate that she would have such problems as an adult? Joann says that it didn't. In fact, she looks back on her early years with a great amount of fondness.

"I grew up in several different places. My dad is a Lutheran minister, so he had churches in a number of places," she explains. "My mom was a homemaker and a part-time substitute teacher. I was born in a little town in northeastern Montana.

"I loved to play and was really active as a kid. We lived in a subdivision where they were doing a lot of building, and all of us kids in the neighborhood enjoyed playing inside the viaducts. We'd make teeter-totters out of planks and bricks, we made up circuses and plays—it was fun.

"In school, I guess I'd be pretty well rounded; I was a good student and I was really active in extracurricular activities, too. Running was my absolute favorite thing. I started running in seventh grade, and I really enjoyed it. I started doing the 220-yard races, then I moved up to the 440. When I was in ninth grade I was racing a halfmile. I was on the cross-country team in high school, and I was always one of the top runners. I even placed in state a couple of years."

Friends in Lots of Groups

Although cliques were common in high school, Joann tried her best to avoid being part of a set circle of friends. Instead, she made friends with people from a wide range of groups.

"I wasn't in the popular clique, but I dated boys who were part of that one," she says, smiling. "I had friends who were athletes, some who were in band, some who were in drama—I guess that was just better for me. I think I was pretty easy to get along with.

"I'm still friends with my best friend from high school, Nancy. She lives in Reno, Nevada, now, but she and her family came here last summer and spent a week with us. That was nice. And through my hospitalizations, when things were really scary for me, she was someone I knew I could call and talk to. Nancy is one of those friends you can not see for years, but when you get together it's as if no time has passed. We're as close as we ever were."

Joann is reluctant to discuss her mental illness. "I know it can make people feel uncomfortable."

A TROUBLED MARRIAGE

Joann focused on nursing in college, and she also became engaged to a young man named Randy. It was a mistake, she says; she should have trusted her instincts at the time.

"I liked him," she replies, "but I wasn't really thinking of marrying him. I don't know why I said yes, or where my heart was at the time. Truthfully? When he proposed, down in the basement of his grandmother's house, I cried. And it wasn't like tears of joy or anything like that.

"I was thinking about some guys I knew, and how becoming engaged meant that those friendships were over. It was like, I'll have to let the relationship with this guy go, and stop being close to that guy—thoughts like that. It wasn't that I had lots of boyfriends. I just wasn't ready to make choices yet. And that's what made me cry.

"He put the proposal inside a fortune cookie," she explains. "And when I read it, I told him I just didn't know. I couldn't give him an answer. That's what I mean about listening to my instincts. Later, I thought to myself, hey, if I really loved Randy, I shouldn't have to think about it, or talk it over with my friends, or anything.

I shouldn't have needed to decide. But I wasn't thinking clearly, I guess, and after a week, I told him I'd marry him."

HE "WASN'T THERE FOR ME"

Joann's first marriage is significant to her disorder, she says, because it was during her six-year marriage to Randy that she had her first breakdown, or "episode."

"There was a lot of emotional abuse I was going through," she explains. "He was a yeller, and anything that went wrong was automatically my fault. I know that I felt very nervous then, very stressed out. I don't know whether the stress triggered the mental illness or caused it—I have no way of knowing that. But I know I was very sad much of the time; my self-esteem was very low.

"Anyway, after college I worked as a nurse practitioner on a reservation in Minnesota. As part of a project, I had been asked to attend a Native American conference in Arizona, which sounded really intriguing to me. Anyway, it was in Arizona that things first changed for me. And as it would turn out, Randy really wasn't there for me at all when I most needed help."

Joann says her first breakdown occurred during her first marriage, a turbulent time in her life.

Maybe an Early Sign

The word *psychosis* indicates a mental state in which a person, among other things, loses his or her sense of reality. Joann's breakdown in Arizona was later described by her doctors as a psychotic episode, and she says the description is apt.

"I lost my sense of what was real, yes," she says. "Although it really hit at this ceremony—a powwow—I believe that maybe there were signs the evening before. I didn't think much about it at the time, you know. I guess that's pretty common with a lot of illnesses. Later, when you look back, you see that there were some symptoms.

"So, the evening before the powwow, I was listening to a speaker. That's what you do at conferences; you listen to a number of speakers. The woman speaking was talking about fear, and I had the oddest sensation that in this crowded setting, she was looking directly into my eyes. I felt as though she had reached down into my belly and twisted it and pulled something out. I know that sounds strange, and I don't mean physically I felt that. But emotionally, I felt a huge impact—very jarring."

Had she ever felt something like that before? Joann shakes her head emphatically.

"Never," she says. "But you know, you can shrug things off. You can say something affected you a certain way because you were hungry, or ill, or too tired, or whatever. And I don't remember actually how I thought about it, but I didn't dwell on it, no."

Drums

The following night was the powwow, and Joann remembers looking forward to it. As soon as the ceremonial drumming started, however, reality seemed to slip.

"Somehow as I listened to the drummers, I felt as though I were hearing something really important in the rhythms," she explains. "Like the ones whose drumming was very even I thought were on the Red Road—that's the life of caring for Mother Earth, being respectful. But there were other drummers I heard who were doing a very uneven, less rhythmic beat. I felt that they must be people who used drugs, who drink. It was very clear to me, although it was not true.

"And as I sat there, I looked at my hand, and it had started swelling. It looked to me to be arthritic, like my grandmother's hand. And that's when I screamed, and people took me outside and tried to help me. I remember I was hearing other voices, too—people from heaven who were calling my name, telling me that I was a great person."

THE DISAPPEARING AIRPORT

Joann was able to get back to her room, with some assistance, and had a restless night.

"I heard screaming in the middle of the night," she says, "and I kept thinking, 'What is going on?' I was frightened, as you can imagine, but it was hard to keep clear in my head of what was really happening and what was unreal. I know I called Randy and told him I was coming home early. I wanted him to meet me at the airport, but he wouldn't. I know that really made me feel bad. I was having severe doubts by then about the marriage, but that was a real wake-up call.

"I called another friend and he said he'd be there to meet me. That was reassuring, but I had more trouble at the airport waiting for my plane. I was experiencing more psychoses—the airport building itself was changing. There was a wall, and then it would disappear. Underneath the old wall, there was a new building with a restaurant and pinball machines. It was as if there were layers, and I could see things change."

Joann says that most upsetting of all was the fear that seized her that the world was ending.

"I felt that unless I could get out of there, I'd be stuck forever in the Arizona desert," she says. "I was scared to death. And every so often, I'd hear the intercom at the airport paging people, except that the names they were calling were all people I knew. I knew that couldn't be. What would all those people be doing in the airport in Arizona?"

GOING TO THE HOSPITAL

Joann has no clear memories of the trip home, but she does recall that she was still very distressed when she got off the plane.

"My friend met me," she says, "and that was good. But I was losing control. I felt like I was in a dream—that's the best way I can describe it. I was seeing things in a different way than I'd ever seen them before, and the meanings seemed so obvious, so clear to me.

"When I was waiting for my suitcases at one of those baggage carousel things, I said to my friend, 'You see how everything is get-

Recalling her first psychotic episode, Joann remarks, "It was hard to keep clear in my head of what was really happening and what was unreal."

ting simpler and simpler? These carousels don't have computers and stuff like the others over there.' It felt like I was really coming up with important impressions, you know? And I think he was very aware that something was wrong, but he just said, 'Yeah, I see that.'

"When we got home, I wasn't there very long. Things happened very fast. I saw Randy and he started talking to me in this voice I'd never heard. It was very evil, very deep. I ran away, down the stairs, but I couldn't get away. The friend who had driven me home told Randy that some weird things were going on, and they figured I needed to go to the hospital. They called an ambulance because it was clear that I was having trouble."

"MY MIND WAS JUST WHIRLING AWAY"

Joann was still convinced that the world was ending when she arrived at the hospital, and she was giving instructions to people as to the best action to take.

"I was saying that it was important to pray to the east, the west, and the north," she says. "Things like that. It wasn't like me to talk that way, either. I mean, some of the spirituality I believe—I have a strong connection with Native American culture. But feeling it and saying it are very different, aren't they? So I was behaving in a different way than I would normally.

"This all happened not too long after the nuclear accident at Chernobyl, in Russia. In my mind, I was sure that I had radiation on me, and that when they took samples of stuff—urine, blood, whatever—they'd find radiation. That panicked me. I know they gave me medication right away to calm me down, but it made me kind of loopy. And I continued to have these random, strange thoughts. It was as if my mind was misfiring, so I couldn't think straight. The thoughts were flying so fast, my mind was just whirling away, and that was both frightening and exhausting."

"LIKE A BUTTERFLY"

Nothing showed up on the tests they did—no drugs, no toxins, and no radiation. The doctors weren't sure what had caused Joann's breakdown.

"They kept me there a week," she says. "I was in a locked ward at first, but after a while I was put in a regular room. Gradually, the thoughts got slower and things got calmer. I went to various therapy groups in the hospital, and that was helpful. Some of the therapy was just talking with other people, and sometimes we worked on projects.

"My mom and dad came to visit me. They were very supportive, but I know now they must have been frightened. They kept a very normal face, though. My dad told me not to be worried, not to be scared. He said that I was like a butterfly, just going through a metamorphosis. That helped, because I'd been feeling so strange, so unhappy."

Years later, Joann's parents told her that when Randy had signed her into the hospital, he listed himself not as her husband but as a friend. "He was embarrassed," she says. "I was having mental problems, and that was an embarrassment for him."

ANOTHER EPISODE

Nearly a decade went by before Joann suffered another breakdown. Since her first episode, she'd been seeing a therapist, and she felt that it was helping. She was also remarried to a man named Joseph and was excited about the birth of their daughter just eleven weeks before. But one weekend, when Joseph was up north fishing, she began experiencing the fearful thoughts that had marked her earlier psychosis.

"I had it in my head that my dad hadn't yet seen the baby," she says. "And I was really worried about it, although there wasn't really anything I should have been concerned about, just worries. So I took the kids and drove there to see my parents. The thoughts, the quick, fast thoughts started happening while we were driving. I was thinking about the end of the world again, and getting more scared all the time.

"I remember driving by a strawberry patch, and thinking that I'd remember where it was, so we'd have something to eat when the world ended. I was thinking about me and the kids picking berries to survive. Anyway, when we got to my parents' house, I was careful not to say any of these things out loud to them or my sister-in-law, who was there, too. I don't think any of them were aware anything unusual was going on."

While picking strawberries Joann remembers a psychotic episode in which she thought her kids could survive on strawberries when the world ended.

"I Told Them We Should Pray"

Although she had been having strange thoughts during the visit with her parents, Joann says that something just popped on the drive home.

"That's the only way I can describe it," she says. "Like it just popped. I got home and there were these two ladies there I didn't really know. They were picking up a car we'd been trying out to see whether we wanted to buy it. Anyway, when we pulled up to the house, I told the women and my kids, who were all very young, about the end of the world. I remember telling them that there were going to be times we'd have to be strong, and other times we'd have to be quiet and loving to one another.

"I told them we should pray, and we did—at least that's how I remember it. Even the ladies [prayed]. But one of them knew my sister—I'm not sure how—and she figured something was weird about how I was acting. So the lady called my sister, and told her she should get over to my house quickly."

Joann smiles sadly. "It was strange because my sister didn't get over to me until the next morning. I'm sure she didn't really know how things were. Anyway, by the time she got there, I had been up all night and I was in trouble. I'd been reading the Bible, thinking those fast thoughts, and worrying. I don't think I slept at all—I remember hearing the birds before it got light, you know? I don't even know if I fed the kids or what. I know that I was eating cilantro from the garden, although I'm not sure why."

Lack of Sleep?

Her sister assessed the situation and knew that Joann needed help quickly. Her first thought was to get in touch with Joann's therapist.

"The therapist knows me pretty well," says Joann. "And she talks to me and thinks that, probably, with the new baby and everything, I'm really suffering from a lack of sleep. I mean, you don't sleep very well in the last weeks of pregnancy, and it doesn't change much when the baby's born. 'So, that could explain the erratic thoughts and behavior,' the therapist said.

"That's the thing I wanted to stress," says Joann earnestly. "See, it's easy looking back and saying, 'Why didn't they catch it?' It's easy in hindsight, you know? But at the time, it could have been something as easy as lack of sleep. It wasn't, of course. I was psychotic, and I know that now. But then, it was explained as something else.

Joann looks forward to spending time with family. Being with family helps her during difficult times.

"Anyway, my sister had a feeling it had to be more than sleep deprivation, especially when I started up again about the end of the world. She just said, very calmly, 'Let's go to the hospital.' And I remember thinking that it was a good idea she had; the hospital was a pretty safe place when the world was ending."

A SEVENTY-TWO-HOUR WATCH

Joann's sister told the doctors to place Joann on a seventy-two-hour watch, which meant that she should be held for that amount of time, no matter how normal she might appear.

"She probably figured that, since I was in the nursing field, I might be able to talk my way out," Joann says, smiling. "And she was worried about what might happen if I left. So I stayed. It was a weekend, and the psychiatrist who was working in that ward wasn't the regular one, you know? He asked me what was going on, and I told him I was thinking about the end of the world.

"He asked me if I thought the world was really going to end, and I said, 'Yeah, I did.' He said, 'You mean, now?' And I told him no, just sometime in the future. So he said OK and figured there was no real problem. I don't think he had a clue why I was there. I

Between bouts with atypical depression, Joann leads a normal life and is able to focus on her family.

wasn't really trying to be manipulative, it's just that at the time he talked to me, I wasn't as frantic-sounding as before.

"At first, the staff let me have a little freedom. I used the whirlpool [and] walked where I wanted to. But when I was taking a whirlpool and listening to a tape on headphones, I kind of zoned out and slid under the water. Well, that got them worried, and I was really monitored after that. I guess they started seeing that I wasn't as fine as they thought I was originally."

A Different Diagnosis

Unlike the first time when her psychotic symptoms went away soon after she was hospitalized, this time Joann continued to have a number of other odd experiences.

"These were frightening, because they tended to be very gory," she says. "I saw nurses during these psychotic episodes who appeared to be covered in blood, head to toe. On the walls I saw Freddy Krueger-like images [the villain in the series of *Nightmare on Elm Street* horror films] that seemed very threatening, very scary. And again, so there's no confusion—none of these things were there, not even remotely. When Joseph came back from his fishing trip, he was very worried, naturally. He stayed there with me for hours at a time.

"On Monday, I was a little calmer, but still hallucinating. I saw a correlation between the light in my eyes and the water I was drinking, and I was sure that if I drank more water the light would become so intense that I would die. It was a relief when the regular psychiatrist came on duty and examined me—I think the staff wanted her to be the one to make decisions on what to do, you know? She asked me about my past history, and I told her about the first episode which had occurred ten years before. I also assured her that I really hadn't had anything like that since—other than a little depression occasionally.

"And again, there was no clear idea what was wrong with me. It's not like with [the] flu or something and it's a no-brainer kind of diagnosis. Because I'd recently had a baby, she wondered if it could be some sort of postpartum depression—that's a fairly common depression with mothers of newborns. But psychosis? I hadn't heard of that with postpartum depression."

Getting On Medication

Joann says that she did learn that one out of a thousand cases of postpartum depression includes some psychotic episodes. Maybe, she thought, that was her problem. But, then, how would that have explained the first episode? She hadn't been a new mother at that time.

"Like I said, it was confusing," she admits. "It was also depressing being in the hospital and being separated from my baby daughter. I'd been nursing her, and with the quick separation, it seemed like we'd been literally torn apart. I missed her, I missed my other kids, and I missed my life."

The psychiatrist asked Joann if she wanted to be put on medication for her depression. She didn't have an automatic response.

"I'd have to stop nursing when I got back home if I decided to take the medication," she says. "See, doctors weren't sure yet what sort of effect the medications might have on a baby, since anything the mother takes ends up in the breast milk. It was something I thought about, but [giving up nursing] seemed [like] a sacrifice I should make. It was better to do that than risk having more of these episodes. So, I went on an antipsychotic medication that day, and she also gave me something that would help me sleep."

HOW LONG?

Not surprisingly, Joann and her husband wanted to know how long she would have to take the medication. She learned that, unlike a case of the flu or a broken collarbone, mental illnesses don't just go away after a period of healing.

"Maybe someday doctors will know as much about [mental] disorders as they do about other illnesses," she says, "and they'll be able to cure them. But *curing* is a pretty rare word with things like depression, psychosis, things like that.

"And that was another reason that I really chose to get on medication. If I chose not to, my chances of staying out of psychiatric wards in the future weren't very good. Once you've had an episode of depression this severe, you have a 50 percent chance of experiencing another. And if you have two episodes, you are 80 to 90 percent more likely to relapse. So at the time, having had two severe breakdowns with psychosis, I was looking at a future that was likely to include more of this stuff.

"And really, even *staying* on medication isn't a guarantee. Lots of people start feeling so much better after they start their medication that pretty soon they figure they don't need it anymore. Then they start having problems. Lots of people also experience unpleasant side effects from various medications—headaches, dizziness. A lot of women find that, while on the medications, they gain weight, and they stop taking it for that reason. I was pretty lucky in that I didn't have too much of a problem.

"So, when Joseph and I asked the doctor how long I'd be on medication, she said she really didn't know. It would take time, she said, to evaluate how it worked, whether the dose needed to be decreased or increased. But what I think is that I'll always be on medication. And while that seems kind of discouraging, the alternative seemed far worse, you know?"

BREAKTHROUGH SYMPTOMS

After Joann was released from the hospital, her life gradually began to balance out. Being on the medication seemed to help, but Joann says that a few times she experienced some of the psychosis symptoms breaking through.

"They weren't as bad as before," she explains. "And I managed to get through them without any trouble, really. Except those times were just scary enough to let me know that something had to change. So what would happen was that my psychiatrist tried some new medications, adjusted some things.

Medication reduces the chances of another hallucination, though, Joann says, "Even staying on medication isn't a guarantee."

"Some of these episodes made me feel paranoid. One time, I remember my mom gave my sister an envelope, and I was kind of worried as to why I didn't get one. I mean, normally, I wouldn't give it a second thought—or even notice it, you know what I mean? But somehow I felt as though I weren't part of whatever was going on, so I kind of demanded, 'Why didn't I get an envelope?' And my mom just said that she'd already given me my pictures. So it was nothing.

"A couple of times I'd get disoriented when I was driving, and that was scary. I'd have these thoughts like 'What if the bridge falls while I'm driving underneath it?' or 'What if someone shoots at me while I'm driving?' Those times, I'd just pray like crazy: 'Please God, just get me home safe, don't let me die.' And then when I got home, I was OK. The symptoms didn't linger or go into something more serious.

"But finally, after a year of being on the medications, I did have another breakdown," she says. "But you know, I have a feeling that it happened because I skipped some doses. My husband and I had gone on a canoe trip with two other friends. I had had fun, but I hadn't eaten much protein. I remember thinking I was looking forward to chicken or something like that after we were done canoeing. And like I said, I think a day or two might have gone by without me taking the pills."

CATATONIC

This third major episode, Joann explains, was unlike the first two. This time, she wasn't talking and thinking rapidly.

"Actually, I was kind of the opposite," she says, smiling. "I was home just sitting on the couch. And I got real glassy-eyed and didn't have anything to say. It wasn't that I was mad, or sad, or anything. I just kind of cut off from things around me.

"Joseph kept trying to talk to me, and I was either not answering or saying something very quietly that didn't make much sense. Anyway, he called the doctor, and it was decided that he would take me in to the emergency room. I remember waiting there a long time, just sitting. And as I sat there, I got more and more cut off, as though I were numb. That's just how I felt—numb.

"The hospital nurses took me upstairs to the psychiatric unit, and I kind of went into a catatonic state. I didn't react to anything. People would talk to me, I guess, but I didn't really understand. I couldn't respond, couldn't do anything. And there's a while where I don't remember much at all.

"But then I woke up or something—I think a day or two had passed. And I was going to go into the bathroom, and this diaper fell off me! And I think, 'Oh my word, I've not been able to get up and use the bathroom on my own!' It was so strange. I guess I was not able to do anything then, like a baby."

GRADUALLY COMING AROUND

Joann explains that her recovery took a little longer because she was refusing to take her medications.

"I'm not sure why," she says. "But I do remember that my mother came to visit after a few days, and she made me take them. See, hospitals can't force you to take medication. But she wasn't taking no for an answer. She literally crammed the pill into my mouth and made me take it!

"Once I got back on the medication, I started feeling better. I'll tell you something, though. I realized how true it is that even when people don't appear to be aware of anything, they can still hear. I remember one of those first days, the nurses taking me to the shower in a wheelchair. I wasn't walking or anything, and they were going to bathe me. I was looking down, just staring at the tiles on the floor. And the nurses were commenting on my long hair. They'd say, 'You've got such pretty hair.' And I could hear them, even though I couldn't answer. I guess hearing is the last sense to go, and I guess I learned that firsthand."

LIVING WITH MENTAL ILLNESS

Joann says that she has been able to come back from that last episode, but there are things in her life that she has had to adjust.

"I did go back to work, but I went back too quickly," she says. "I mean, I took a month off after I got out of the hospital, but I should have gone in for an hour or two, just gradually at first. I work as a women's health practitioner, and I was anxious to get back. But it was too soon. I started feeling a little odd.

"See, at that point, I guess I didn't really know enough about my illness to understand the symptoms well enough. I was stressed out because I was coming back to a full schedule, and that was wrong."

Do her coworkers know the nature of her illness? She shakes her head.

"No, they know I was hospitalized, but I haven't really told any details. And the reason is what I was saying before. People aren't as understanding about things like this as they would be with a different sort of illness like depression. So rather than deal with that, I'd rather keep it to myself. Or talk about it with people who understand.

"Anyway," she says, "I've learned to take care of myself. I am far more organized about my medications—I'm like a little old lady with her pill containers marked for every day of the week. That way, I can tell at a glance if I took it or I just intended to take it and forgot. When you get busy, that can happen. And I'm also very careful not to get too tired out. I can tell—and my family can, too—that I start going a little too fast when I get tired. That's when it's time to take it easy, and I've learned to do that."

"NO GUARANTEES"

Living with any illness can be more bearable if one has things to look forward to, and Joann has many. She puts a high value on the time she spends with her children and her husband.

"Our friends have a cabin up north," she says, "and our two families are going to go up together. That will be fun. I'm also going to take my oldest daughter to New York in May. We're going to go see my goddaughter's graduation. We're really looking forward to that. We'll get to see her off to her prom, too. I look forward to working in the garden and having our bathroom remodeled. These aren't big things, but to our family they're important."

Joann pauses for a moment and says, "You know, I was thinking that I'm a good example of how you can never tell how things will turn out, just thought of that from what I was saying a while ago about how I'm a pack rat. Anyway, it reminded me of stuff I have down in the basement—the high school graduation program listing me as valedictorian, pictures from band concerts, [and] ribbons and stuff from track meets."

She widens her eyes as if she just remembered something. "Oh, did I tell you that I was the Junior Miss Montana runner-up?" she asks. "I was, and I've got that stuff downstairs, too. And pictures somewhere of the homecoming court when I was a senior.

"I guess what I'm saying is that, back in high school, it might have looked like I was really destined for a great life—or at least an easy one. It seemed like I was lucky, you know? Like I had what it takes. But if there was anything I'd want other people to know about having a mental illness, or brain disorder—call it whatever you want—I'd say that there are no guarantees. I mean, here I am, with stuff like I'm going through. I don't know if I'll have another psychotic episode or when. But it's not just something that only happens to other people. It can happen to anyone, I guess."

Megan

"[I HAD] A FEELING OF SHEER
TERROR THAT IF I DIDN'T DO
THINGS A CERTAIN WAY, OR IF I
FAILED TO REMEMBER TO DO
SOMETHING IMPORTANT,
EVERYTHING WAS JUST GOING TO
FALL APART."

Megan is paging through a book, looking for something.

"Here it is," she says. "Right here, it's kind of a checklist, a lot like the psychiatrist went through with me the first time I saw him. You kind of add up your 'yes' answers and it gives you a real good indication of whether you have OCD."

OCD or obsessive-compulsive disorder, is what Megan was diagnosed with several years ago, and what continues to affect her life in a number of ways. Standing in the living room of her parents' home, Megan does not look like someone with any sort of disorder. A lively, interesting young woman in her mid-twenties, she seems totally at ease with herself and her surroundings.

"IT WAS 'YES, YES, YES, AND YES'"

She points to the first question in the diagnostic test.

"See, like here," she reads, "'Do you wash your hands more than twelve times per day?' "And this one: 'Do you find yourself counting things for no reason?' And here," she says, "my personal favorite: 'Do you touch switches on electric devices several times and count, despite trying not to?'

"When the psychiatrist was going down the list, asking me questions like these, it was 'yes, yes, yes, and yes.' I pretty much knew already that I had the disorder, and those were some of the symptoms. At that first appointment, I told him that I thought I had obsessive-compulsive disorder. And I remember him looking up and saying, 'Boy, you sure do have it.'"

She laughs dryly. "I don't know if it was good to be right or not in a case like that. But in a way, it really did feel good—after suffering for so long without telling anyone—to finally be able to talk to someone about it."

OBSESSIVE AND COMPULSIVE

The disorder, Megan explains, has two parts. An obsession is a thought that gets out of hand.

"It might start out as wondering if you turned out the lights before you left home," she says. "That's a pretty common thing. But while a normal person would either say to themselves, 'Yeah, I turned them off,' or if they weren't sure, check and make sure, the person with the obsession would think about it over and over.

"Even when I check the lights, I'd question whether I'd made a mistake, like they might still be on. And I'd check again. That's the compulsion part, where you deal with the obsession by checking and rechecking and rechecking because you really aren't sure.

"It isn't just about turning off lights. It can be worrying about locking the door, or unplugging an iron, or putting a stamp on a letter, anything. There are obsessive-compulsive people who are obsessed with the idea that they have germs on their hands from touching certain things, and as a result, they end up washing their hands fifty times, one hundred, even three hundred or more times a day."

NO SENSE

Megan says it's important that people know that everyone occasionally worries that they have forgotten to do something. That doesn't mean they have OCD.

"I wouldn't think anything of it if a friend said she had to go back and check to make sure she locked her door," says Megan. "But if she went back and then went back a second and a third time, I might worry. And see, that's the hardest part about it: People with OCD know very well that what they are experiencing sounds odd.

"I mean, I was very, very secretive about it. I didn't want to look like I was crazy because I was aware that what I was doing wasn't right. It wasn't normal. Nobody I knew did things like that. And I really felt like I needed to hide it—and that was depressing, too."

HIGH SCHOOL DEPRESSION

Megan's disorder probably began in high school, but she insists that the signs were pretty vague. Besides, she says, she was dealing with other problems back then.

A psychiatrist diagnosed Megan with obsessive-compulsive disorder when she was in college, though she thinks her disorder began in high school.

"See, I suffered from depression in high school," she explains. "I really felt isolated. Not the typical rah-rah traditional high school happiness that I guess we're supposed to feel. I was an introvert—still am. I was an only child, grew up around lots of adults, watched public television, way different than anyone else.

"I enjoyed doing projects on my own, I enjoyed being with my family. I really never wanted to do things in groups. I did work in the drama department doing costumes, and that was fine. I liked being behind the scenes. But I had kind of a 'Don't look at me, don't talk to me' attitude. Anyway, the depression was kind of the consuming thing for me. I felt that I wasn't connected, and it made me really depressed.

"But I do remember having kind of an irrational need to make sure my locker was locked. I say 'irrational' because there was almost nothing in it. A notebook, maybe. So why it was such a big thing, I didn't really know. But I'd pull on it, checking, and pull again. Looking back, yeah, I see it was the beginning of OCD for me. But it wasn't a worry then. It would be, but not until later."

A NIGHTMARE JOB

The summer after graduating from high school, Megan got a job at a nearby hotel as a housekeeper.

"I was really having trouble—something that seemed so strange to me," she says. "I'd be in these rooms and I'd start worrying about the electrical things that were plugged in. I'd worry that they weren't plugged in properly and, as a result, there'd be a fire. The whole place could burn down, and it would be my fault for not checking the plug.

"I mean, I knew very well that the clock radio was not going to catch on fire. But there was a lot of checking and rechecking, and I was really baffled as to why I was being so strange about it. I didn't know the term *obsessive-compulsive*. I didn't know of anybody who had such a disorder or anybody who acted the way I was feeling. All I knew is that I was so tense, so worried, that the job was a nightmare. It was every day, every room I was in.

"I finally quit. I just went in one day and made up some silly excuse as to why. I couldn't tell my parents—are you kidding? How do you explain something like that?"

Megan stops for a moment. "You know, I remember something about one night when my dad came to pick me up at the hotel after work. I was riding home—it had been a particularly awful shift—and I remember thinking to myself that I just would really like to

Megan says she has always been an introvert. During high school, she recalls, "I felt that I wasn't connected, and it made me really depressed."

be put away in an institution somewhere, where I wouldn't have to feel responsible for anything. Just to get away. But then I thought, I can't ever get away, because no matter where I was, even if there were no windows, nothing on the walls, there'd always be something I could obsess about. At that moment, I just knew that it was true. And that was a really, really sad thought."

AN INSIGHT

However, when she went away to college that fall, Megan found herself really enjoying it. The feeling of being isolated and alone that had plagued her through high school did not follow her. Her checking and worrying were only small problems, and she seemed to be able to handle them.

"I had friends [and] I was taking a lot of interesting classes," she says. "I took a psychology class my freshman year, and it was an eye opener. The professor talked a lot about various mental illnesses and disorders, and one of them was obsessive-compulsive disorder, OCD. I was amazed. I felt as though he was going through my head, reading my mind! At last, I had a name for what I was sure I had, what had made my summer job such a nightmare.

"And even though I was enjoying college, I knew I was still having the problems with checking and worrying. Not necessarily to the extent of the previous summer, but they were there. And now, after hearing the professor talking about it, I was hoping I could start working on curing the OCD."

She smiles. "But if I thought that knowing the name of a disorder was the same as curing it, I was wrong," she says. "I went to my counselor at school, and I told him the problems I'd had, and how it had really become a bigger problem for me—checking doors, lights, stuff like that. I told him that I knew something wasn't right about what I was doing.

"And you know what he said? He said, 'Oh, you're such a creative person, I bet you could tie bows on things instead of checking them!' That was his big suggestion. And I thought, 'Boy, you don't really have any idea at all what I'm talking about, do you?'"

TROUBLE AS A HOUSE SITTER

Giving up on trying to work with the college counselor, Megan struggled on her own. She kept her obsessions secret, hiding her behavior from her friends. She was successful most of the time, but it was becoming more and more stressful as time went on.

"Sooner or later, I knew it would attract attention," she says. "I just had a feeling that I'd get into some situation that would be too much for me. And I was right. It happened during the summer. I guess that was lucky in a way, because the college campus is pretty deserted during the summer, so there weren't people around to notice.

"Anyway, I had a job in the library, and some studio space—I was an art major, and that was a big deal. It was even a better deal because I was going to be house-sitting for a professor I really, really respected, someone in the art department. He was traveling, and rather than have his house sit empty, he was letting me use the space. I was looking forward to the summer, but it turned out to be a really bad experience.

"It started out OK—I mean, I was kind of nervous about the house, locking up, making sure everything was safe. But really, you couldn't say I was actually *living* in the house; I mean, I never used the kitchen. I was so afraid I'd leave the oven on or a burner or something. [I] didn't even want to go near the kitchen. [I thought] I'd do something that would start [a] fire [or] blow up."

"EVEN BRUSHING UP AGAINST A CURTAIN"

It wasn't only the kitchen, either. The whole house began taking on a potential for danger.

"The whole place was really neat, and all white—everything just so orderly, so immaculate," Megan says. "And that's not the way I live. Not that this professor expected me to, but I felt that I had to keep things neat every minute. I was afraid to spill, afraid that it would become dirty or stained.

"Even brushing up against a curtain became dangerous. I remember thinking, I moved the curtain a little, and what if it catches in the door and then the door wouldn't shut? And then maybe a burglar would come and steal stuff, and it would be all my fault. And again, I was aware of how outrageous it all sounded. It sounded that way to me, too. But the feelings were there."

"EVERYTHING WAS JUST GOING TO FALL APART"

What were the feelings exactly? Megan says they can be summed up in a single word: panic.

"It was pounding heart, fast breathing, scared panic," she says. "A feeling of sheer terror that if I didn't do things a certain way, or if I failed to remember to do something important, everything was just going to fall apart. I used a curling iron, and I was [always] sure I had left it on. It got to the point where I actually had to carry the curling iron with me, take it in my hand and walk out the door holding on to it; otherwise, I was panicky, imagining it was on and was going to start the house on fire.

"It was almost like I believed that it would plug itself back in. Absurd thoughts like that, but they made me panic. And really, there were sometimes that it wasn't even necessary to think of a

Hiding her compulsive behavior from her friends became increasingly difficult, Megan says.

particular disastrous outcome. It was almost an automatic terror, just generally being obsessive.

"There was no one on campus to tell, no one that could help me," she says. "And like I said, I'd kept it from my family for years, so there was no one that knew. But things were really coming to a head. I was soon at the point where I was literally frozen, unable to do anything in the house but sit in a chair. I couldn't leave, couldn't go to work, couldn't even use the house. And I was miserable."

"WAS I TURNING INTO SOMEONE LIKE THAT?"

Finally, Megan made the phone call she had not wanted to make. She called home and told her parents that she was in trouble. She was crying and embarrassed, and was unable to go on.

"Plus, I had this job I was supposed to be going to," she says, "and I didn't know how I was supposed to get there when I was afraid to leave the house. I knew about OCD, but I really didn't know what to do about it. I'd still never heard of anyone famous or anything who had it—just case histories, you know? Like in a textbook, where a doctor says, 'Jimmy came in to my office, and his hands were red and bloody from washing them five hundred times,' stuff like that. And they sounded odd, and for all I knew they were goofy looking—you just imagine what they're like. They must be just plain crazy. And that frightened me: Was I turning into someone like that?

"But anyway, I told my parents I didn't know what to do, and they drove down to the college. They were very supportive. My dad—I think he might have even guessed, although I'm not sure. But you know, my dad is a minister, and at one time he was a hospital chaplain. I think he was used to seeing certain behaviors and was observant in that way, although he had never spoken about it with me.

"My mom was a different story. She was completely thrown by what I told her. She felt confused and—I don't know—bewildered by it. She felt guilty, too. She wondered how she had missed seeing that in me, and the fact I'd been suffering and she hadn't known. So until she read about it [and] learned more, she felt really uncertain."

"HE KNEW JUST WHAT TO DO"

But that day, when she called home, her parents came right away—and that in itself was comforting.

"Actually, my dad was really good in that situation," Megan remembers. "He knew just what to do. We went to the hospital, saw a triage nurse at the mental health ward, and she got me set up with an appointment the next day with a psychiatrist. And that was the biggest relief of all! To go so long without talking about something, and finally get to talk with someone who isn't horrified by it, who has seen it a lot—that was really a good feeling.

"Once that all happened, my parents basically helped me get through the rest of the summer. They took turns staying with me at night, so I wouldn't have to be afraid of the house and all the responsibility. One or the other would stay until I went off to work, and then I'd be OK.

"Then in the evening, my mom or dad would come drive back to the college and help me with the house again. It allowed me to finish the job, and also kept me from letting the professor down. I mean, I had promised to take care of the house, so I couldn't just leave and go home."

NO THERAPY

Megan's first encounter with the psychiatrist was a positive one. After talking about OCD and going through the checklist of symptoms, he explained that there were two ways to approach life with the disorder.

"There were medications I could take that would help me deal with the panic, with the nervousness," she says. "And he gave me a prescription for Prozac. The other approach was therapy, and he didn't push that part of it, and I was relieved. I'm not interested in therapy at all, I've never had it, never want to do it. It's just the kind of person I am. Give me a book to read or a list of things I should do, and I'll work on those things. But I don't want to do therapy. I'm an introvert; I prefer to be on my own.

"One of the things I learned about OCD was that it was a real disease, a disorder. I mean, it wasn't my behavior or anything that was causing these obsessive thoughts. It's a chemical problem, something in the circuits or connectors that isn't working right. I think of it like, you have a message in your brain that's supposed to go to another part of your brain. The message is maybe 'Did I turn out the lights?' And the receiving end is supposed to say, 'Yes, you turned them off.' And you're supposed to go on with your business.

With support from her parents, Megan was finally able to seek help for her disorder.

"But in my brain, there's a roadblock there. Not just a road-block—there's a whole rioting crowd saying, 'You did not check the lights; check them again!' I'm being besieged by these—I don't want to say voices, because I'm not hearing voices—but these thoughts. And there's no way around this barrier. And it's amazing. I've seen brain scans of people who have OCD, and you can see very clearly how much energy is being used in their thought patterns versus someone who doesn't have the disorder. The thoughts are coming and coming and coming, without any relief."

NO MAGIC CURE

Megan admits that therapy has been shown to help people with OCD, usually by teaching them to ignore the barriers that block the normal thought patterns.

"It's like they show you a door, and you're allowed to check it twice, but no more than that," she says. "And later, [you can check it] only once. It's like weaning you off the need to check over and over. So, neither therapy nor medication can make those thoughts go away, not really. But they can help you ignore them, or at least deal with them, for as long as you are doing the therapy or taking the medication. I don't think now there is anything that can magically cure you of OCD to the point where you take some pill or something and after that you are free of obsessive thoughts and compulsions. Maybe someday, but not now.

"But anyway, I took the Prozac, and it helped me be calmer. Once the school year started, things weren't so bad because I wasn't on my own, being responsible all by myself. I worked in the art studio at night, but I was sharing it with others, and I just made sure I wasn't the last one to leave, so that was fine. And I did tell my roommate finally, and she was really supportive. So I was pretty good, and definitely calmer."

DISAPPOINTMENTS

Megan says that her problems began again after graduating from college. She began graduate school at a large university far from home, but it wasn't at all what she'd hoped.

"I hated it," she says. "I admit I was comparing it to college, but it just wasn't a good place for me. Lots of infighting among the faculty, and it would sort of spill over on the students. Just a toxic environment—that's the best way I can explain it. It's ironic. After having such a miserable time in high school, I really enjoyed college. It was the first time I realized I could enjoy friendships and doing things with other people instead of projects on my own all the time.

"And so after this great college experience, here I was in a place where I felt lonely and isolated. I didn't have much in common with anyone I met. I was depressed, I really was. I stayed away from the studio quite a bit, which is not the best thing for an art student! And the OCD came back, but part of that was really my own doing because I had stopped taking the medication."

SIDE EFFECTS

Her decision to stop taking Prozac had nothing to do with graduate school, Megan says.

"It was that I was having really unpleasant side effects from it," she explains. "It started back before leaving college. I'd get really, really dizzy sometimes. And as it got worse, there were times when I was very close to blacking out. It was scary, and when I got to graduate school, I worried about blacking out when I was driving or something. And so on my own, I kind of started weaning myself off the medicine, a little at a time. I was on a pretty high dose, so I just decreased it gradually."

Why didn't she go to her psychiatrist and see whether there was a different medication that worked better? Megan shakes her head.

"I did go to a new psychiatrist when I was down in Illinois in grad school," she says. "I had my records transferred down there. I thought it made sense since I couldn't drive all the way home to see the other guy when I was that far away. But I didn't care for this new guy—he really pushed therapy. I told him several times that I preferred not to do it that way, but he was really insistent. So no, I really didn't want to continue with him. So, it seemed like the time to get off the medication.

"I didn't notice any real severe problems with the OCD right away," she insists. "Prozac is one of those drugs which I understand stays in your system for quite a while even after you've stopped taking it. But after a while, I started having trouble, just like before. And this time, I was on my own, too far away for my parents to drive back and forth taking care of me."

AT THE BANK

One of the ways Megan earned money while in graduate school was doing some nighttime computer processing at a local bank. That became a source of frustration for her.

"I was the only one there at night," Megan explains. "I was supposed to lock up when I left. It was only two doors, and it should have taken me only a couple of minutes. But the obsessive thoughts

During graduate school, Megan, an art student, began to feel depressed and her condition became more severe.

had returned, and the compulsions. I easily spent an hour just checking and rechecking the doors.

"The only good thing was that you had to set an alarm when you did the doors, and you only had a short time to get outside once the alarm was set; otherwise, it would trigger the police to come. So, at least I got as far as outside before I started obsessing. I worried that the door wasn't locked, even though I just did it. So I'd stand there and pull on it a specific number of times to convince myself that it was locked.

"Then I'd walk around the corner of the building to the other door and check that one, the same way. I had blisters on my hands from pulling on the doors, rattling them. And I'd be sore in my arms and shoulders, too. That's because of being so tense, so tight, you know? It was the panic, combined with the inability to believe that the doors were locked."

"I'D SIT IN MY CAR AND CRY"

Sometimes Megan would try to convince herself that the doors were locked and get in her car, but she was still uneasy, and usually got back out and began the process over again.

Checking and rechecking the locks on doors is one of the obsessions associated with Megan's disorder.

"It was a ritual. I guess I didn't say that before," she explains. "I had a particular stance, my feet had to be just so. I mean, it wasn't the same ritual for everything. Like, if I was worried about one door, I might stand with my right foot ahead of the other one. And I'd say, 'OK, I'm checking this door, so I have to keep this position.' Or if it was a clock radio or something, I had to torque myself around, going over my shoulder to do it. No matter what, I'd have to do it by the routine I established.

"Another thing—there are particular numbers that are, I don't want to say lucky, exactly, but sort of charmed or something. So, the ritual of it seems like it might work as long as I do it that many times—maybe fifty or sometimes one hundred. For me, I used the numbers starting with two or seven, then ten. And then it's multiples of those, I guess.

"But anyway, I can remember just being so tired, so burnt out and frustrated. I'd sit in my car after being there an hour or more and [was] still no more convinced that the place was locked than I was at first. And I'd sit in my car and cry, feel really depressed. That was one of the real low times."

Coming Home

Megan says that she couldn't wait to leave graduate school. She was depressed, and her OCD had become more severe. She no longer felt that she could handle living on her own.

"I came home," she says simply. "I also got back on medication. Not the same one, so the dizziness and the fear of blacking out aren't a problem. But I'm in a job where I'm working fifty-plus hours a week and it got to the point where I was so stressed about it—plus being tired. I just thought, things are getting out of hand.

"I work for a health group; I'm in the recruitment services area. I line up job fairs [and] connect with colleges to do recruiting for jobs here. I set up those programs. I'm good on the phone, and much of my work involves phone work. But it's a lot of extra things that come up, and I feel like I'm doing stuff no one else has the time to do. And the OCD, like I said, that was coming back. Not that it was ever gone—it's just that I was able to work past it. But I wasn't able to do that anymore. The thoughts had become too invasive."

Megan's obsessions became exhausting and extremely frustrating, prompting her to quit graduate school. "I came home. I also got back on medication."

"Are the Things on My Desk Arranged Right?"

"At work, the problem wasn't locking doors—not this time," Megan explains. "Instead, I was becoming obsessive about the alignment of things on my desk. I was really particular that everything had to be just so. The first thing I thought of when I walked into my office was, 'Are the things on my desk arranged right? Is this cord touching this piece of paper?' That was totally unacceptable for me. No cords could touch.

"I know a lot of it was thinking about starting fires. And of course I know that a telephone cord touching a notebook or an envelope is not going to ignite, [but] in my mind it was a constant threat. For the same reason, I would never turn my lights on in my office, not even on the most cloudy, drab days. People would stick their heads in my office and ask, 'Why are you sitting in the dark?' I'd just shrug and say, 'Oh, I just like it like this,' or something.

"So even with the medication, I still check the desk alignment over and over. I don't panic—the medication helps that aspect of it—but the checking goes on. It's not just at work either, there's always something else that becomes a problem, something I have to check over and over."

Things Change

Megan says that something that has surprised her about the disorder is that its focus changes occasionally.

"It's funny, there'll be something I need to check, something I obsess about, and it will go on for months and months. And then it will kind of diminish, and something else will come up that I'd never really checked before.

"Like right now, I've got this thing with the car doors. I have to check the driver's side door and the one behind it, ten times each. It's strange, because I don't even consider the other side of the car; I don't seem to be worried about those two doors at all. I mean, people could be lining up on the passenger side of the car to break in or whatever, but it doesn't appear to be a problem for me!"

She laughs at herself. "Oh, and the emergency brake. I check that a number of times. I was just thinking today that I was probably going to break the stupid thing since I'm checking it so much. But I know that it will go away, or there will be a day when I'll forget to do it and

86

I'll realize, 'Oh, I'm supposed to check that.' And it will just taper off. But something else will always be there to take over the obsessive part. I can't remember ever having a time when there was no obsession—not since I've had OCD."

FOR THE LONG HAUL

Does she think her OCD will ever go away? Megan thinks a moment, but says she guesses that it won't.

"I'd love it if I woke up one morning and there were no thoughts about checking things," she says. "Maybe someday there will be a breakthrough and doctors can pinpoint what it is that causes the OCD. But I don't really hold out much hope for that happening very soon.

"I *have* heard that for some people, OCD diminishes as they get older. So maybe that will happen to me later on. But I'm pretty young, so it's not happening anytime soon. I'm on different medication, like I said, and it helps somewhat. The only unpleasant side effect is that my hands kind of tremble. It can be a little embarrassing; like at work, it makes me look as though I'm nervous. But I am not complaining. It's far better than blacking out.

"I also am seeing a different psychiatrist, and he's really neat. Kind of an older guy, really interesting. He likes to talk about traveling or things he's done. I mean, we talk a lot before he even gets around to asking about my OCD. That's nice, you know? Less clinical. So I see him regularly to make sure the dosage of the medication is OK."

"I CAN'T SAY 'NEVER'"

Megan admits that she is resigned to OCD being a part of her for the rest of her life. And that means living at home with her parents, in the same house she grew up in.

"I know there's a real stigma about adult kids living at home," she says. "But my mom and dad love having me here, and I know they have no plans to kick me out. Plus, to tell you the truth, I know I couldn't handle living on my own again. It was so awful in grad school, and with the stress of my job, and the OCD on top of that, I need to be here. I like coming home and having someone to talk to. I need the stability."

Can she envision a time when she would leave? To get married, perhaps, and raise a family? She considers this a moment.

"I can't say 'never.' I don't know, I'm not sure," she says honestly. "It would have to be someone who is really sensitive to what I go through, completely aware of who I am. Keep in mind, even on medication, it takes me two hours to get out of the house in the morning. It would be hard to imagine someone that would be able to handle that! But I guess you never know. It might happen someday."

"MY LIFE ISN'T SO BAD"

Even with the limitations she faces, Megan is—at least on the outside—a confident young woman. She says that, even among OCD sufferers, she is quite lucky.

"I was reading the other day about a man who had OCD back thirty years ago or something," she says. "He wasn't so much into checking things, as I am. He was more obsessed with germs, getting contaminated from things. And as you can imagine, obsessions about germs can be just as irrational as my obsessions about telephone cords suddenly bursting into flames on my desk, right?

"Anyway, this guy was wealthy, but all his money couldn't help him. He became so imprisoned by the OCD that he lived in one room, everything sealed up, so no germs could get to him. He had his servants or whoever do all the compulsions—putting plastic on the windows, washing things down hundreds of times. But they were still his compulsions. And reading about that kind of thing, I felt sad for him, but very lucky.

"I have a job, I have people I see at work. I travel sometimes, and although it's sometimes stressful, I've been able to handle it. I have parents who are understanding."

She smiles. "Really, my life isn't so bad."

Epilogue

It has been several months since these individuals were interviewed, and in that time there have been some changes in their lives.

Joann has had no problems with her depression or the medication. She had an active summer, going to a blues festival and taking a canoe trip with her daughters in the wilderness. She has promised herself for years that she will get her bathroom remodeled and is now excited that it is going to happen.

Megan is still leading a quiet life, but has gone on some picnics with friends. She and her family enjoyed time at their cabin this summer. She acknowledges that the obsessive-compulsive symptoms are still part of her life, but says she is coping well.

Bruce has not had an easy time. A few months ago, his father (who had been quite ill) passed away, and his ex-wife, who is still a good friend, has been battling breast cancer. Perhaps because of such stressful situations in his life, he had two manic episodes recently, both of which resulted in his being hospitalized for some time. His medicine, which seemed to have worked for years, was changed, and he is adjusting to it. His daughter Pam says that it was difficult to see her father being belligerent and angry when that is not his true personality. "I'm just so happy he's out of the hospital now," she says. "I'm looking forward to just going on a walk with him down by the lake."

Mike's caseworker is unsure of his whereabouts.

Ways You Can Get Involved

THE FOLLOWING ORGANIZATIONS
CAN PROVIDE MORE DETAILED
INFORMATION ON VARIOUS ASPECTS
OF MENTAL ILLNESS.

American Psychiatric Association
1400 K Street NW
Washington, DC 20005
(888) 357-7924
www.psych.org

Representing more than 38,000 psychiatric physicians around the world, the APA's vision is a society where diagnosis and treatment of mental illness are available and accessible to all. The APA's website offers up-to-the-minute news on political and social issues affecting mental illness, as well as updates on medical research.

National Alliance for the Mentally Ill
Colonial Place Three
2107 Wilson Boulevard, Suite 300
Arlington, VA 22201
(703) 524-7600
www.nami.org

NAMI is dedicated to the eradication of mental illness and to the improvement of the quality of life of all people affected by mental illnesses. A nonprofit agency, NAMI provides education about mental illness, supports increased funds for research, and advocates for better health benefits, better housing, and more accessible rehabilitation for people with mental illness.

National Resource Center on Homelessness and Mental Illness
345 Delaware Avenue
Delmar, NY 12054
(800) 444-7415
www.nrchmi.com

This organization provides technical assistance, identifies and synthesizes knowledge, and disseminates information about homelessness and mental illness. It runs workshops and training sessions, develops referral lists, and provides bibliographies of information that will help workers in both fields.

For Further Reading

Scott Barbour, ed., *Schizophrenia*. San Diego, CA: Greenhaven Press, 2002. Excellent background on causes, symptoms, and treatment of this illness.

Terry Spencer Hesser, *Kissing Doorknobs*. New York: Delacorte Press, 1998. Fictional account of a fourteen-year-old who develops obsessive-compulsive disorder, and the effect it has on her family.

Patricia McCormick, *Cut*. Asheville, NC: Front Street, 2000. Also fictional, about a girl in a residential treatment facility. Excellent insights into the challenges of teen mental illness.

Barbara Moe, *Coping with Mental Illness*. New York: Rosen, 2001. A helpful explanation of several mental illnesses, with a good index.

Victoria Sherrow, *Mental Illness*. San Diego, CA: Lucent Books, 1996. Good information on the need for understanding within the community, and the difficulties people have after being in hospitals and other care facilities.

Index

American Psychiatric
   Association, 6
atypical depression, 52–54

bipolar disorder
   Bruce's experiences with,
      12–14, 26–31
   Nick's experiences with, 6
   research money spent on, 8
Bruce
   describes bipolar disorder,
      12–14, 26–31
   enters a care center, 23–24
   experiences with depression,
      16–17
   grows up on a farm, 14–15
   jobs held by, 23–25
   leaves state hospital, 22–23
   moves to the city, 18–19
   as a student, 15–16
   time spent in hospitals by, 17,
      19–21

care centers, 23–24
clinical depression, 6

depression
   Bruce's experiences with,
      16–17
   Joann's experiences with,
      52–54
   Marci's experiences with, 6
   Megan's experiences with,
      73–74
   see also atypical depression;
      clinical depression

DNA, 9

Gale (Bruce's cousin), 16, 24–25
Gordie (Bruce's friend), 16

hospitals
   Bruce's experiences in, 17,
      19–23, 29–30
   Joann's experiences in, 63–65,
      68–69
   Mike's experiences in, 42–44
Hyman, Steven, 9

Jessie (Bruce's daughter), 27, 29
Joann
   breakdowns of
      first, 56–60
      second, 60–65
      third, 68–69
   childhood of, 54
   decides to take medications,
      65–67
   describes atypical
      depression, 52–54
   friends of, 54
   marriages of
      to Joseph, 61
      to Randy, 55–56, 58–60
   returns to work, 69–70
Joseph (Joann's husband), 61,
   67–68

Klonopin, 46–48
Krueger, Freddy, 65

Marci, 6

Marge (Bruce's wife), 24–26, 28–30
medications
  improvements in, 7, 9
  Joann decides to take, 65–67
  taken by Bruce, 17
  taken by Megan, 80–81
  taken by Mike, 46–49
Megan
  attends college, 75–76
  describes obsessive-compulsive disorder, 71–73, 77–78, 82–84, 86–87
  jobs held by, 74–77, 82–83, 85
  returns to parents' home, 85, 87–88
  seeks help, 79–81
  starts graduate school, 81–82
mental illness
  cures for, 10
  defined, 6
  as a misunderstood disease, 7
  number of people suffering from, 6–7
  public's view of, 7–8
  scientific progress in understanding of, 8–9
  see also names of specific illnesses
Mike
  describes schizotypal personality disorder, 32–34, 43
  experiences of, in high school, 37–40
  experiences of, in the marines, 34–37
  discharged, 37, 40
  friends of, 40
  interest in art, 50
  jobs held by, 50–51
  lives in parents' home, 40–41
  medications taken by, 46–49
  run–ins with the police by, 41–42, 44–46

time spent in hospitals by, 42–44
Monroe, 8
muscle relaxants, 21

Nancy (Joann's friend), 54
Nicholson, Jack, 21
Nick, 6
Nightmare on Elm Street (film), 65

obsessive-compulsive disorder (OCD)
  Megan's experiences with, 71–73, 76–78, 82–84, 86–87
  Monroe's mother's experiences with, 8
OCD. See obsessive-compulsive disorder
One Flew over the Cuckoo's Nest (film), 21

Pam (Bruce's daughter), 27
postpartum depression, 65
Prozac, 80–82

Randy (Joann's husband), 55–56, 58–60
Ron (Mike's friend), 40

schizophrenia, 6, 8–10
schizotypal personality disorder, 32–34, 43
shock treatments, 21
state hospitals
  Bruce's experiences in, 19–21, 29
  Mike's experiences in, 42–44
suicide, 17

Thorazine, 17
tranquilizers, 7
Trent, 6

University of Pittsburgh, 9

About the Author

Gail B. Stewart is the author of more than eighty books for children and young adults. She lives in Minneapolis, Minnesota, with her husband Carl and their sons Ted, Elliot, and Flynn. When she is not writing, she spends her time reading, walking, and watching her sons play soccer.

Although she has enjoyed working on each of her books, she says that *The Other America* series has been especially gratifying. "So many of my past books have involved extensive research," she says, "but most of it has been library work—journals, magazines, books. But for these books, the main research has been very human. Spending the day with a little girl who has AIDS, or having lunch in a soup kitchen with a homeless man—these kinds of things give you insight that a library alone just can't match."

Stewart hopes that readers of this series will experience some of the same insights—perhaps even being motivated to use some of the suggestions at the end of each book to become involved with someone of the Other America.

About the Photographer

Carl Franzén is a writer/designer who enjoys using the camera to tell a story. He works out of his home in Minneapolis, where he lives with his wife, three boys, two dogs, and one cat. For lots of fun, camaraderie, and meeting interesting people, he coaches youth soccer and edits a neighborhood newsletter.